Essential
Prague

AAA Publishing 1000 AAA Drive, Heathrow, Florida 32746

Prague: Regions and Best places to see

 Best places to see 34–55

 Featured sight

 Staré Město Area 83–106

 Josefov and Beyond 134–146

 Hradčany, Malá Strana and Beyond 107–133

Nové Město and Beyond 147–163

Original text by Christopher and Melanie Rice
Revised and updated by Michael Ivory

Edited, designed and produced by AA Publishing
© AA Media Limited 2011

Published in the United States by AAA Publishing,
1000 AAA Drive, Heathrow, Florida 32746.
Published in the United Kingdom by AA Publishing.

978-1-59508-410-1

Colour separation: AA Digital Department
Printed and bound in Italy by Printer Trento S.r.l.

A04658
Maps in this title produced from mapping © MAIRDUMONT/Falk Verlag 2011
and © ISTITUTO GEOGRAFICO DE AGOSTINI S.p.A., NOVARA 2010
Transport map © Communicarta Ltd, UK

About this book

This book is divided into six sections.

The essence of Prague pages 6–19
Introduction; Features; Food and drink; Short break

Planning pages 20–33
Before you go; Getting there; Getting around; Being there

Best places to see pages 34–55
The unmissable highlights of any visit to Prague

Best things to do pages 56–79
Places to have lunch; stunning views; best pubs; speciality shops and more

Exploring pages 80–163
The best places to visit in Prague, organized by area

Excursions pages 164–183
Places to visit out of town

Maps

All map references are to the maps on the covers. For example, Karlův most has the reference ✚ 10K – indicating the grid square in which it is to be found.

Admission prices

Inexpensive (under 100Kč)
Moderate (100Kč–250Kč)
Expensive (over 250Kč)

Hotel prices

Room per night:
£ budget (under 2,500Kč);
££ moderate (2,500–4,000Kč);
£££ expensive to luxury (over 4,000Kč)

Restaurant prices

Three-course meal per person without drinks:
£ budget (under 500Kč);
££ moderate (500–1,000Kč);
£££ expensive (over 1,000Kč)

Contents

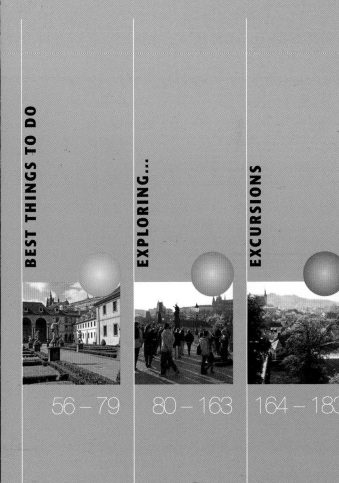

BEST THINGS TO DO

EXPLORING...

EXCURSIONS

56 – 79   80 – 163   164 – 183

The essence of...

It is easy to get to know Prague, even to feel at home here. To enjoy the city to the fullest, be prepared to abandon your sightseeing itinerary whenever the mood takes you – the galleries and museums can wait. Put away the map and wander off the beaten track. Don't neglect the side streets and courtyards, where Prague is often at its most beguiling. To see more, take the tram rather than the metro, and be prepared to go the extra mile: climb to the top of that hill – no city in Europe has more rewarding views.

features

Praguers know their minds and have always been willing – though not always able – to express them. Standing in Old Town Square, one is reminded of the great Czech religious reformer, Jan Hus, who took on the might of the Catholic Church in order to stand up for what he believed. As so often in the nation's history it was an unequal, albeit heroic, struggle. More than 500 years later, in January 1969, a university student, Jan Palach, suffered a horrific death by setting himself on fire rather than acquiesce in the Soviet invasion.

Politicians, of course, prefer to leave permanent monuments in brick and stone – the Klementinum, the Charles Bridge, the Wallenstein Palace, Obecní dům. Everywhere you walk in Prague, its buildings are reminders of the city's history; but they are also aesthetic statements by the architects, artists and sculptors who contributed so much to this most beautiful city. Prague is much more than a glorified museum, however; it is a dynamic place, where individuals are allowed, even encouraged, to stand out from the crowd. To get a true feel for the city, spend time in the pubs and cafes that poke out of every nook and cranny. For the traditional view, head for U zlatého tygra (► 18, 63), a spit and sawdust pub. Just as representative, however, of today's Prague is Radost FX (► 163), a meeting

place for young people from around the world. Cosmopolitan and receptive to new ideas, Prague is now more irresistible than ever.

GEOGRAPHY

● Prague lies on the River Vltava at 50 degrees 5 minutes north and 14 degrees 25 minutes east – the heart of Central Europe. The lowest point is 176m (577ft) above sea level, the highest 396m (1,299ft). Prague is 292km (181 miles) from Vienna, 350km (217 miles) from Berlin, 1,037km (644 miles) from Paris and 1,237km (768 miles) from London.

POPULATION

● Prague covers an area of 497sq km (192sq miles), about two-thirds that of New York, but its population is only 1.2 million, compared with New York City's 8 million. Fewer than 30,000 people (2.5 per cent) live in the historic core of the city; the overwhelming majority inhabit apartment blocks known as *paneláks*, on the outskirts. Some 95 per cent of the population is of Czech nationality.

TOURISM

● Every year approximately 8 million tourists visit the Czech Republic, mostly from Germany, America and Britain, although more and more Italians, Russians and Japanese are now visiting the country. Tourism makes up more than 5 per cent of the country's GNP.

ENVIRONMENT FACTS AND FIGURES

Prague has:
● 10,000ha (24,710 acres) of green space
● 31km (19 miles) of rivers, 10 islands, 17 bridges
● 750,000 road vehicles
● 3,400km (2,112 miles) of road
● 59km (37 miles) of metro line with 57 stations.

food & drink

You can be sure of one thing when you eat out in Prague – or anywhere else in the Czech Republic, for that matter: you will not go hungry. All the national dishes are incredibly rich and filling.

MEAT AND VEG

Czech cuisine is heavily meat-based. Pork, beef and chicken are all standard fare – but the pig is king. Popular dishes include pork with dumplings and *kyselézelí* (pickled cabbage), roast duck with bacon dumplings, and roast beef with a sour cream sauce. *Wiener schnitzel*, known to the Czechs as *smažený řízek*, is another favourite. In expensive restaurants, you can buy game – venison, pheasant, hare or even wild boar. Most meat is boiled or roasted and served in gravy and accompanied by potatoes or dumplings *(knedlíky)*.

Fresh vegetables, other than the ubiquitous pickled cabbage, are appearing on menus with increasing frequency. On nearly every menu you'll find *šopský salát* – sometimes called *balkánsky salát* – which is a small bowl of chopped olives, bell peppers and

cucumbers in a sweet vinegar with a salty white cheese shredded liberally on top. Most restaurants also offer several side dishes at the end of the menu: small plates of vegetables, pasta, potatoes or rice. Vegetarians should note that many apparently meatless dishes are cooked in animal fat. The best advice is to declare yourself at the outset: *Jsem vegetarián (-ka* for the feminine form). Or ask for a meal *bez maso* (without meat).

Of the fish dishes, boiled carp served in melted butter, roasted pike, fillet of trout cooked in a green pepper sauce and smoked salmon are all delicious.

Try to leave some room for a dessert such as apple strudel or plum dumplings.

BEER

Czech beer *(pivo)* is justifiably famous and is fully appreciated by the Czechs themselves – the Republic boasts the highest per capita consumption in the world: 157 litres (34.5gallons) annually. Plzeň produces the clear golden nectar known as Pilsner Urquell abroad and locally as Plzeňský Prazdroj. Gambrinus is another common brand. The other main centre of beer production is the southern Bohemian town of České Budějovice, Budweis in German. Don't be misled by the name – the American beer, Budweiser, and

the Czech brew, Budvar, have nothing in common. These large, national beers are delicious, but smaller, local beers can be just as good. If you fancy trying a dark *(tmavé)* beer, head for U Fleků (► 62–63), which produces its own brand.

WINES AND SPIRITS

Most Czech wine is produced in the warmer, more sheltered parts of southern Moravia and is consumed locally, rather than exported. The best of the red wines is Frankovka or Svatovavřinecké – Tramín is a reliable white variety. The Mělník region, just north of Prague, produces a small amount of wine of variable quality (sometimes none at all, if the weather is bad). A dry white wine known as Rulandské bílé is probably the best, and can often be found on menus. There are three types of liqueur worth sampling: Borovička, a fiery, juniper-flavoured spirit with the impact of gin, which should be treated with the same respect; Slivovice, a plum brandy; and, best of all, the wonderfully aromatic Becherovka, a herb-based 'health' drink concocted in the 19th century by a pharmacist in the spa town of Karlovy Vary.

short break

If you have only a short time to visit Prague and would like to take home some unforgettable memories, you can do something local and capture the real flavour of the city. The following suggestions will give you a wide range of sights and experiences that won't take very long, won't cost very much and will make your visit very special. If you only have time to choose just one of these, you will have found the true heart of the city.

● **Listen to the buskers** on the Charles Bridge (► 89) throughout the day while browsing the many stalls for souvenirs or art.

● **Watch the Twelve Apostles**
signal the hour as they emerge
from the Astronomical Clock in
Old Town Square (➤ 46). The
first figure to emerge is that of a
skeleton, representing Death,
followed by the Twelve Apostles.
The clock not only gives the time
but also shows the signs of the
zodiac and seasons as well as the
course of the sun.

● **Take the funicular** to the top
of Petřín Hill (➤ 122) to enjoy spectacular views
of both the castle complex and across the river
and beyond.

● **Admire** Mucha's stained-glass window in St.
Vitus's Cathedral.

● **Take tram 22** on its scenic journey through the
Malá Strana and up to Hradčany. The tram runs
from Vinohrady through Nové Město and then
across the river to Malá Strana, ending at the
Hradčany area.

● **Take a walk up Wenceslas Square** (➤ 52–53)
stopping to look at Josef Myslbek's famous
equestrian statue of St Wenceslas and the
small shrine to the martyrs of the Communist era.
St Wenceslas is flanked at the foot of the
monument by statues of four other saints: Ludmila,
Adalbert (Vojtěch in Czech), Procopius and Agnes.
The Square became the focus for demonstrating
Praguers and has been the scene of both tragic and
joyous events in the city's history – most recently,
the Velvet Revolution of 1989, which drove out the
Communist regime.

● **Visit U zlatého tygra** (➤ 63), a traditional Czech pub, where guests sit at plain wooden tables and wait to be served glasses of the frothy Pilsner Urquell lager. It's noted as one of the top three pubs in Prague, so make sure you get there early as seats fill up quickly.

● **See the Picassos and Van Goghs** in the Veletržní Palace (➤ 54–55). Built in 1928, this huge building has six floors all accessible by lift (elevator) and is a treasure house of modern European art.

● **Visit the wonderful art nouveau confection, Obecní dům** (➤ 155). Built as a civic centre in the early 1900s, it has undergone complete renovation. The Smetana Hall on the first floor is the city's most pleasant concert hall and is where the opening concert of the Prague Spring Music Festival is held each year.

● **Listen to some Mozart** – at the Estates Theatre (➤ 97) or starring puppets at the National Marionette

Theatre (➤ 146). The Estates Theatre hosted the premiere of Mozart's *Don Giovanni* in 1787 and this opera can still be seen here today or alternatively performed by puppets at the National Marionette Theatre.

● **Enjoy the peaceful surroundings** of the Royal Gardens (➤ 75, 116–117). Reached from the lovely Belvedere or from the Powder Bridge to the north of the castle, they were created by Ferdinand I in 1534 to include fountains and manicured lawns.

Planning

Before you go

WHEN TO GO

JAN	FEB	MAR	APR	MAY	JUN	JUL	AUG	SEP	OCT	NOV	DEC
−1°C	0°C	4°C	9°C	14°C	17°C	19°C	18°C	14°C	9°C	4°C	0°C
30°F	32°F	39°F	48°F	57°F	63°F	66°F	65°F	57°F	48°F	39°F	32°F

🌥 High season ☁ Low season

Temperatures are the average daily maximum for each month.

Prague has hot summers and bitterly cold winters. May and June and then September and October are the best times to go, although Prague's winter snow can be great, with the concert and opera seasons at their height. Go in spring to see the wonderful show of blossoms on the fruit trees of Petřín Hill and avoid the oppressive heat of summer. However, January to March and November are the best times to go if you want to avoid the hustle and bustle of tourist crowds.

Autumn is a lovely time to visit when the days are still bright with sunshine but the crowds have dwindled. Come in freezing winter to visit the winter markets and join the New Years' crowds in the streets.

WHAT YOU NEED

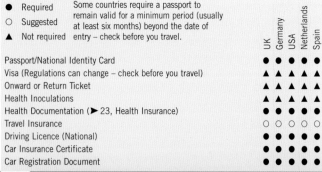

	Required	Some countries require a passport to remain valid for a minimum period (usually at least six months) beyond the date of entry – check before you travel.	UK	Germany	USA	Netherlands	Spain
●	Required						
○	Suggested						
▲	Not required						
Passport/National Identity Card			●	●	●	●	●
Visa (Regulations can change – check before you travel)			▲	▲	▲	▲	▲
Onward or Return Ticket			▲	▲	▲	▲	▲
Health Inoculations			▲	▲	▲	▲	▲
Health Documentation (►23, Health Insurance)			●	●	●	●	●
Travel Insurance			○	○	○	○	○
Driving Licence (National)			●	●	●	●	●
Car Insurance Certificate			●	●	●	●	●
Car Registration Document			●	●	●	●	●

WEBSITES
- Prague Information Service: www.prague-info.cz
- City of Prague Official Guide: www.welcometoPrague.cz

TOURIST OFFICES AT HOME

In the UK
Czech Tourism UK, Scotland and Ireland, 13 Harley Street, London W1G 9QG
☎ (020) 7631 0427;
www.czechtourism.com

In the USA
Czech Tourism USA, 1109–1111 Madison Avenue, New York, NY 10028 ☎ (212) 288-0830

In Canada
Czech Tourism, 2 Bloor Street West, Suite 1500, Toronto, Ontario M4W 3E2
☎ (416) 363-9928

In Australia
Czech Embassy, 8 Culgoa Circuit, O'Malley, ACT 2606, Canberra
☎ (02) 6290 1386

HEALTH INSURANCE
All visitors to the Czech Republic are advised to carry comprehensive health insurance. While EU nationals with a European Health Insurance Card (EHIC) are entitled to free medical care in the Czech Republic, this will give no choice over treatment nor cover the cost of repatriation should this prove necessary.

Dental treatment must be paid for. Emergency 24-hour care is available at Palackého 5, Nové Město, Praha 1 (tel: 224 946 981).

TIME DIFFERENCES

| GMT | Prague | Germany | USA (NY) | Netherlands | Spain |
| 12 noon | 1PM | 1PM | 7AM | 1PM | 1PM |

The Czech Republic is on Central European Time (GMT+1), but from late March, when clocks are put forward one hour, until late October, Czech Summer Time (GMT+2) operates.

NATIONAL HOLIDAYS

1 Jan *New Year's Day*
Mar/Apr *Easter Monday*
1 May *May Day*
8 May *Liberation Day*
May/Jun *Whit Sunday and Monday*

5 Jul *St Cyril and St Methodius Day*
6 Jul *Jan Hus Day*
28 Sep *St Wenceslas Day*
28 Oct *Independence Day*

17 Nov *Student Demonstration of 1989*
24–25 Dec *Christmas Eve/Christmas Day*
26 Dec *St Stephen's Day*

WHAT'S ON WHEN

19 January *Jan Palach Day:* The country marks the day in 1969 when 20-year-old Charles University student Jan Palach died after setting fire to himself (on 16 January) on Wenceslas Square to protest against the invasion by Warsaw Pact troops the previous August, and subsequent Soviet occupation of Czechoslovakia.

February–March *Opera Musical Theatre Festival:* Held in odd-numbered years. Focuses on Czech opera. Venues include both the National Theatre and the Estates Theatre.

30 April *Witches' Night:* A bonfire held on Petřín Hill celebrates the traditional end of winter and the birth of spring.

May and early June *Prague Spring:* A three-week event of classical music and dance, performed in churches, palaces and concert halls around Prague. The celebrations begin with a procession from Smetana's grave in Vyšehrad to his namesake concert hall in Obecní dům.

Mid–late May *Czech Beer Festival:* More than 50 brews and the best of Czech cooking and entertainment provided for up to 10,000 guests at the Letňany Exhibition Grounds.

Late May and June *Fringe Theatre Festival Prague:* This is a week of indoor and outdoor performances around the city by drama, music, comedy and dance troupes.

Late September and October *Prague Autumn Music Festival:* Three weeks of classical music performances by orchestras and musicians from around the world. Performances take place at the Rudolfinum.

Late September *Vinohrady Grape Harvest:* An annual celebration of the country's first grape harvest takes place in two main squares in the neighbourhood that was home to the Royal Vineyards during Charles IV's reign. Traditional music and crafts along with plenty of *burčak* – the sweet but potent young wine.

November *International Jazz Festival:* For almost 30 years Prague has hosted this week-long festival of performances by jazz legends from the United States to Ukraine, with plenty of local stars in between.

17 November *Anniversary of the Velvet Revolution:* A commemoration and wreath-laying ceremony conducted on Wenceslas Square and at the Velvet Revolution memorial at Národní 16.

December *Christmas market on Old Town Square:* Every festive season a giant Christmas tree lights up the centre of the square, while the space around it is crammed with market stalls selling carved toys, bobbin lace, ceramics, glass figurines, Christmas ornaments and tasty gingerbread cakes, barbecued sausages and *svarak* (mulled wine). Entertainment is provided by street performers.

Getting there

BY AIR

Ruzyně Airport

20km (12 miles) to city centre

🚋 N/A

🚌 30 minutes

🚗 20–40 minutes

Prague's international airport is Ruzyně Airport (tel: 220 113 314), which has all the modern amenities you would expect of a European airport.

Czech Airlines – ČSA (tel: 239 007 007; www.csa.cz) operates direct

scheduled flights to Prague from Britain, mainland Europe and North America. Flight time from London is 2 hours. Prague is connected by rail to all main European capitals (➤ 28, Getting around). Other international carriers that fly into Prague include BA, Delta Airlines, KLM, Lufthansa and Air France, as well as budget airlines such as EasyJet, Ryanair and Wizz Air.

Ruzyně Airport is 20km (12.5 miles) from the city centre and a 20- to 40-minute journey depending on your mode of transport.

Airport taxis are expensive, but AAA taxis are reasonably priced and have English-speaking operators (tel: 222 333 222).

The next best method into town is on a Cedaz minibus (tel: 221 111 111), which run every 30 minutes between 5:30am and 9:30pm and will drop you at the Náměstí Republiky for around 120Kč per person. Cedaz will also take you or your whole party to your hotel for a reasonable set charge of a few hundred crowns. Look for the booth signed 'City Centre 120Kc'.

If you don't have a lot of luggage take the No 119 bus from the airport to Dejvická metro station. From there, take the main A-line into the city centre. This service runs daily from 5am to midnight, as do the buses.

BY RAIL

The overnight train from London – via Brussels and Cologne (information: tel: 840 112 113; www.cd.cz – Czech only) arrives at Hlavní nádraží (Main Station), which is on the C (red) metro line. Inside the station there is a tourist information office, ATM machines, exchange facilities and a 24-hour left-luggage office. It is a short walk from Václavské náměstí (Wenceslas Square). Many international trains also arrive at Prague's other main station – Nádraží Holešovice. A useful website for European rail travel is www.seat61.com.

BY BUS

International and national bus services arrive at Florenc bus and metro station on the east side of the city. The Old Town is a 15-minute walk, or the B and C metro lines can take you anywhere else you want to go.

BY CAR

Prague is well integrated into the European motorway network. The D-1 motorway connects the city to Brno, Bratislava and points south and east. The D-5 links Prague to Plzeň, Nuremberg, Munich and the west. The D-8 motorway connects Prague with Dresden and Berlin to the north.

Getting around

PUBLIC TRANSPORT

Internal flights Czech Airlines (ČSA, V celnici 5, Praha 1; tel: 239 007 007; www.csa.cz) links Prague with Brno, Ostrava and Karlovy Vary.

Trains Czech Railways (České Dráhy; tel: 840 112 113, 24 hours; www.cd.cz) links major towns and many other points of interest, though some destinations (eg Karlovy Vary) are more easily reached by coach. Services range from slow trains stopping at every station *(osobní)* to ultra-fast tilting Pendolinos (Supercity) connecting Prague with Brno and beyond. Always check which of the Prague stations is served by your train.

River boats From April to September cruise boats ply the Vltava river, as far as Troja Château in the north of Prague and Slapy Lake in the south.

Urban transport Prague is a compact city and easy to walk round. In bad weather or for travel over longer distances reliable public transport is available with a fully integrated system consisting of underground railway *(metro)* , tram *(tramvaj)* lines and bus *(autobus)* routes. The three lines of the metro, A (green), B (yellow) and C (red) are clean, fast and safe. Trains run 5am to midnight, at 2-minute intervals during peak hours, 5 to 10 minutes at other times. The letter 'M' with a downward arrow marks station entrances. Tram lines fan out from the city centre, connecting with bus routes serving the suburbs. Trams run at 10- to 15-minute intervals, more frequently in the peak hours, and there is a limited night service. Route 22 is particularly useful for tourists, running through the historic central quarters of the city and calling at Malostranská metro station before climbing the Castle hill. Here there are stops at Královský letohrádek (Royal Summer Palace), Pražský hrad (Prague Castle) and Pohořelec (for Strahov Monastery and the upper part of the Hradčany district), see www.dpp.cz/en.

FARES AND CONCESSIONS

There is one ticket for the metro, tram and bus. Buy tickets at *tabaks*, newspaper kiosks, metro stations and some tram stops (look for the yellow machine): they cost 26Kč single, 13Kč child. Day passes are also available (1 day: 100Kč; 3 days: 330Kč; 5 days: 500Kč; 3- and 5-day passes include the ticket price of an accompanying child). Failure to produce a valid ticket will result in a 950Kč fine (700Kč on the spot).

The Prague Card is a 4-day tourist pass providing entry to Prague Castle, most of the city's major museums and historic buildings (excluding the Prague Jewish Museum) and, for a bit more, unlimited travel on the metro, trams and bus. An adult card with transport is 1,120Kč, or 790Kč without. Buy cards at Prague Information Service Offices (➤ 30). For further information, see www.pis.cz/en.

Holders of an International Student Identity Card (ISIC) are entitled to a 50 per cent reduction on admission to Prague's museums.

TAXIS
Prague taxi drivers have a poor reputation, but AAA, ProfiTaxi and City Taxi are reliable. You have the right to request a printed receipt.

DRIVING
● A car is not necessary or advised in Prague as much of the city is off-limits to cars and parking is by permit only.
● If you're heading out of town, car rental is easy to arrange, but can be expensive. Shop around as local firms may be cheaper. Try Dvořák Rent-a-Car (tel: 224 826 260) or Europcar (tel: 224 811 290).
● Driving is on the right.
● Speed limit on motorways (annual toll payable): 130kph (80mph); minimum limit: 50kph (31mph); on country roads: 90kph (56mph); on urban roads: 50kph (31mph).
● Seat belts must be worn in front seats – and rear seats where fitted.
● Under 12s may not travel in the front seat.
● *Don't* drink *any* alcohol if driving. Penalties are severe.
● Unleaded petrol comes as *natural* (95 octane) and *super plus* (98 octane); the latter is available only at larger petrol stations. Diesel *(nafta)* is also available. In Prague, filling stations are few and far between, but some open 24 hours.
● If you break down, ÚAMK, the Czech automobile club, operates a 24-hour nationwide breakdown service (non-members pay in full), tel: 1230 or 261 104 123. On motorways use emergency phones (every 2km/1 mile) to summon help.

Being there

TOURIST OFFICES
Czech Tourist Authority
- Vinohradská 46, 12041 Praha 2
- ☎ 221 580 111
- www.czechtourism.com

- Staroměstské náměstí, Praha 6, Old Town ☎ 224 861 476

Prague Information Service
(Pražská informační služba PIS)
- Staroměstská radnice (Old Town Hall), Staroměstské náměstí, Praha 1
- ☎ 221 714 444
- www.prague-info.cz
- 🚇 Daily 9–7 🚊 Staroměstská

- Hlavní nádraží (Main Railway Station) Wilsonova, Praha 2
- 🚇 Mon–Fri 9–7, Sat–Sun 9–4
- 🚊 Hlavní nádraží

- Malostranská Mostecká vez, (Lesser Town Tower), Mostecká, Praha 1
- ☎ 257 530 487
- 🚇 Apr–Sep daily 10–10; Oct, Mar 10–9; Nov–Feb 10–6
- 🚊 Malostranská

- Rytířská 31, Praha 1, Old Town
- 🚇 Mon–Sat 10–6, Sun 12–6
- 🚊 Staroměstská

MONEY
The monetary unit of the Czech Republic is the Koruna česká (Kč) – or Czech crown – theorectically divided into 100 haléř, though haléř coins are no longer in use. There are coins of 1, 2, 5, 10, 20 and 50 crowns. Banknotes come in 50, 100, 200, 500, 1,000, 2,000 and 5,000 crowns. Money may be changed at the airport, in banks, major hotels, Čedok offices, and in the centre of Prague at exchange offices. Exchange offices advertising 'No Commission' are usually a poor place to change money.

TIPS/GRATUITIES

Yes ✓ No ✗		
Hotels	✗	
Restaurants	✓	10%
Cafes/bars	✓	10%
Taxis	✓	10%
Porters	✓	40Kč
Toilets	✓	7Kč

POSTAL AND INTERNET SERVICES

Post offices have distinctive orange *Pošta* signs. The main post office (Jindřišská 14, Nové Město, Praha 1) is open daily 24 hours. There are several branches in the city which are open 8am–7pm (noon Sat) and closed Sun (tel: 221 131 111, non-English speaker).

Internet cafes are scattered around Prague. Rates are high, about 1Kč per minute. Some cafes and bars offer free WiFi, but connection can be patchy. Better hotels offer in-room internet or public WiFi connection.

TELEPHONES

There are public telephones on the street and near metro stations. You may find a few odd coin phones about, but most operate on prepaid telephone cards *(telefonní karta)*. Buy cards (200 and 300Kč) from post offices, *tabaks*, grocery stores and newsagents. Country code: 42, Prague city code: 02.

Emergency telephone numbers

Police: 112 or 158	Fire: 112 or 150
Ambulance: 112 or 155	

International dialling codes

From Czech Republic to:	USA: 00 1
UK: 00 44	Netherlands: 00 31
Germany: 00 49	Spain: 00 34

EMBASSIES AND CONSULATES

UK ☎ 257 402 111	Netherlands ☎ 233 015 200
Germany ☎ 257 113 111	Spain ☎ 233 097 211
USA ☎ 257 530 663	

HEALTH AND SAFETY

Sun advice The sun is not a real problem in Prague. June to August is the sunniest (and hottest) period, but there are often thunder showers to cool things down. If the summer sun is fierce, apply a sunscreen and wear a hat, or visit a museum.

Drugs Pharmacies *(lékárna* or *apothéka)* are the only places to sell over-the-counter medicines. They also dispense many drugs *(leky)* normally available only by prescription in other Western countries.

Safe water Tap water is perfectly safe but heavily chlorinated, so it can have a metallic taste. Bottled water is available everywhere: *né perlivá* is still water, *jemně perlivá* is lightly carbonated and *perlivá* is carbonated.

Personal safety Prague is a comparatively safe city, though petty crime is prevalent in central areas. Report any loss or theft to the *městská policie* (municipal police) – black uniforms.

● Watch your bag in tourist areas, and on the metro/trams, especially trams 22 and 23.

● Deposit your passport and valuables in the hotel safe.

● Never leave valuables in your car.

ELECTRICITY

The power supply in the Czech Republic is 220 volts. Plugs are of the two-round-pin variety, so an adaptor is needed for most non-Continental European appliances and a voltage transformer for appliances operating on 100–120 volts.

OPENING HOURS

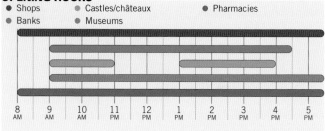

● Shops ● Castles/châteaux ● Pharmacies
● Banks ● Museums

Some shops close for lunch but most open all day. At weekends, usual hours are Sat 10–7 and Sun 10–5. Grocery stores *(potraviny)* open from 7am; department stores and large shopping centres open until 8pm or 9pm. Outside Prague centre, shops are usually closed on Sunday except for malls in the suburbs. Some pharmacies open 24 hours. Museums and art galleries usually open from 10–6; they are closed Mondays. Castles and other monuments open daily (except Monday) May to September and weekends in April and October, but may be closed at other times.

LANGUAGE

The official language of the Czech Republic is Czech *(čeština)* – a highly complex western Slav tongue. Czech sounds and looks daunting, but apart from a few special letters, each letter and syllable is pronounced as it is written – the key is always to stress the first syllable of a word. Any attempt to speak Czech will be heartily appreciated, although English is spoken by many involved in the tourist trade. Below are a few Czech words that may be helpful.

yes	*ano*	sorry	*pardon*
no	*ne*	help!	*pomoc!*
please	*prosím*	today	*dnes*
thank you	*děkuji*	yesterday	*včera*
good morning	*dobré ráno*	tomorrow	*zítra*
goodnight	*dobrou noc*	open	*otevřeno*
excuse me	*promiňte*	closed	*zavřeno*
room	*pokoj*	toilet	*záchod/WC*
I would like a room	*potřebuji pokoj*	bathroom	*koupelna*
... single/double	*... jednolužkový/*	shower	*sprcha*
	dvoulůžkový	room number	*číslo pokoje*
how much per night?	*kolik stojí jedna noc?*	key	*klíč*
bank	*banka*	free (no charge)	*zdarma*
post office	*pošta*	more	*více*
foreign exchange	*směnárna*	less	*méně*
how much?	*kolik?*	the bill	*účet*
restaurant	*restaurace*	lunch	*oběd*
coffee house	*kavárna*	dinner	*večeře*
fixed-price menu	*standardní menu*	dish of the day	*nabídka dne*
airport	*letiště*	tram	*tramvaj*
train	*vlak*	ticket	*lístek*
train station	*nádraží*	... single/return	*jednosměrný/*
metro station	*stanice*		*zpáteční*
bus	*autobus*	... first/second class	*první/druhá třída*

Best places to see

1

Chrám svatého Mikuláše (St Nicholas's Church)

www.psalterium.cz

The all-powerful Jesuit Order commissioned this superb church, the ultimate expression of Prague baroque, at the beginning of the 18th century.

Restored at a cost of 120 million Czech crowns, this monumental building was constructed between 1704 and 1756 by father-and-son team,

Christoph and Kilián Dientzenhofer, and completed by Kilián's son-in-law, Anselmo Lurago. The interior decoration builds on an accumulation of *trompe l'oeil* effects, culminating in *The Apotheosis of St Nicholas* by Johann Kracker, a fresco covering more than 1,500sq m (1,795sq yds) of the nave ceiling. The splendid dome is 18m (59ft) higher than the Petřín Tower. But not everything is as costly as it appears. Many of the mottled pink and green pillars and other details are *faux marbre*, while the four more than life-size statues under the dome are made of wood, with a surface covering of glazed chalk. These dramatic characterizations of the Church Fathers include a vigorous St Cyril triumphantly lancing the devil with his crozier. The sculptor, Ignaz Platzer, also created the copper statue of St Nicholas, which looks down from the high altar. Also of note is the rococo pulpit, with its angels and cherubs, made by Peter and Richard Práchner in 1765. The baroque organ, played by Mozart in 1787, boasts 2,500 pipes and 44 registers. Four years later it was played at a funeral Mass in his memory. The church was full, evidence of the esteem in which he was held.

✚ 8K ✉ Malostranské náměstí, Malá Strana, Praha 1
🕐 Mar–Oct daily 9–5; Nov–Feb daily 9–4. Concerts Wed–Mon at 6pm 💰 Inexpensive; concerts expensive
🍴 Cafes (£), restaurants (££–£££) nearby 🚇 Malostranská
🚌 Malostranské náměsti

2 Josefov and Zidovské Museum v Praze

www.jewishmuseum.cz

The Jewish Museum administers most of the surviving monuments of the former ghetto, poignant reminders of the many centuries of Jewish life in Prague.

Jewish people first settled in the Old Town in the 12th century. In 1254 the area was surrounded by a ghetto wall, following a decree of the third Lateran Council. The ghetto was a centre of learning, with its own Talmudic school and Hebrew printing press. Although Prague's Jews were regularly subjected to discrimination and persecution, wealthy elders, like Mayor Mordechai Maisel in the 16th century, won privileges for the ghetto by placing their wealth at the disposal of the imperial treasury. In 1784 Emperor Joseph II relaxed many restrictions, and in 1849 Josefov (as the Jewish quarter was now called) was incorporated into the city. Most of the ghetto slums were demolished at the end of the 19th century. The Holocaust all but wiped out the Jewish population of Prague – only around 1,500 registered Jews now live here.

Hitler planned a museum in Josefov recording the history of the 'extinct' Jewish race. Ironically, this ensured the preservation of treasures and furnishings confiscated from synagogues all over Bohemia and Moravia, and many of these items form the basis for exhibits on display across the six main sights that form the Jewish Museum (► 58). These are the newly restored Spanish Synagogue; the Klausen Synagogue (► 136–137), the Maisel Synagogue (► 138), the Ceremonial Hall (► 140), the Pinkas Synagogue (► 140–141), a particularly poignant Holocaust memorial, and the Old Jewish Cemetery (► 143). Also in the care of the museum is the oldest functioning synagogue in Europe, the Old-New Synagogue (► 142), the focus of worship since the 13th century,

✚ 12J ✉ U Staré školy 1, Josefov, Praha 1 ☎ 222 749 300 🕓 Apr–Oct Sun–Fri 9–6; Nov–Mar Sun–Fri 9–4:30. Closed Jewish hols 🖐 Expensive. A combined ticket for all sights is available 🚇 Staroměstská 🚌 Pravnická fakulta or Staroměstská

3 Katedrála svatého Víta (St Vitus's Cathedral)

www.hrad.cz

St Vitus's took nearly six centuries to complete and was consecrated only in 1929, yet it stands on the site of a chapel founded in 925.

Work started on the present Gothic building in 1344, under the direction of Matthias of Arras. Architect Petr Parléř and his two sons were responsible for the lofty choir and the surrounding chapels, which were finally completed early in the 15th century. The tower on the south side was given its Renaissance steeple in 1562, to which baroque embellishments were later added. The nave and the impressive west end date from the second half of the 19th century. The Golden Portal (the original entrance) on the south side contains a mosaic of the Last Judgement, dating from 1370, which has been restored to its former glory.

The Chapel of St Wenceslas, dating from 1358 to 1367, is one of the oldest parts of the building and the most beautifully decorated. The lower walls are encrusted with scintillating jasper and amethyst, while the frescoes (14th–16th centuries) depict scenes from the passion of Christ and the life of St Wenceslas (the saint is buried directly underneath the chapel). The foundations of the 11th-century Romanesque basilica were unearthed as the cathedral was nearing completion and can be seen in the crypt, along with the sarcophagi of the kings of Bohemia. King Vladislav Jagiello commissioned the beautiful Royal Oratory in the 1480s: the vaulted ceiling, shaped like the branches of a tree, is highly unusual. An exquisite silver funerary monument to the cult saint, John of Nepomuk, was erected in the choir in 1736. One of the cherubs points to the saint's tongue, which was said never to have decayed. The cathedral also contains fine 20th-century stained glass, notably Alphonse Mucha's portrait of saints Cyril and Methodius in the third chapel from the west end.

✠ 7J ✉ Pražský hrad, Hradčany, Praha 1 ☎ None
🕐 Apr–Oct Mon–Sat 9–5, Sun 12–5; Nov–Mar Mon–Sat 9–4, Sun 12–4 💵 Free; moderate charge for crypt, tower and choir 🍴 Cafe (£), restaurants (££–£££) within castle complex 🚇 Malostranská 🚊 Pražský hrad

4 Loreta

www.loreta.cz

This pretty baroque shrine has been a place of pilgrimage since 1626, when it was endowed by a Bohemian noblewoman, Kateřina of Lobkowicz.

The Loreta shrine was inspired by a medieval legend. In 1278, so the story goes, the Virgin Mary's house in Nazareth was miraculously transported by angels to Loreto in Italy and thus saved from the Infidel. The Marian cult became an important propaganda weapon of the Counter-Reformation and, following the defeat of the Protestants at the Battle of the White Mountain in 1620, some 50 other Loreto shrines were founded in Bohemia and Moravia.

The heart of the Loreta is the Santa Casa, a replica of the Virgin's relocated house. Sumptuously decorated, it incorporates a beam and several bricks from the Italian original. On the silver altar (behind a grille) is a small ebony statue of the Virgin. The rich stucco reliefs, depicting scenes from the lives of the prophets, are by Italian artists.

The much larger Church of the Nativity was designed by Kilián Dientzenhofer between 1734 and 1735, with ceiling frescoes by Václav Reiner and Johann Schöpf. Less edifying are the gruesome remains of saints Felecissimus and Marcia, complete with wax death masks. The cloisters, originally 17th century but with an upper storey added by Dientzenhofer in the 1740s, once provided overnight shelter for pilgrims. In the corner chapel of Our Lady of Sorrows is a diverting painting of St Starosta, a bearded lady who prayed for facial hair to put off an unwanted suitor, only to be crucified by her father whose plans for her wedding were thwarted. The Loreta treasury has a famed collection of vestments and other religious objects, including a diamond monstrance (receptacle for the consecrated host) made in Vienna in 1699, which glitters with a staggering 6,200 precious stones.

✚ 5J ✉ Loretánské náměstí 7, Hradčany, Praha 1 ☎ 220 516 740 🕐 Tue–Sun 9–12:15, 1–4:30 💰 Moderate 🚇 Pohořelec

5 Pražský hrad (Prague Castle)

www.hrad.cz

Dominating Hradčany with majestic assurance, Prague Castle has a history stretching back more than a thousand years and is still the Czech State's administrative centre.

The Castle's château-like appearance dates from 1753 to 1775, when the Empress of Austria, Maria-Theresa, ordered its reconstruction, but the Gothic towers and spires of St Vitus's Cathedral are clues to a much older history. Many misfortunes took their toll, culminating in a disastrous fire in 1541 which engulfed Hradčany. Extensive restoration work resulted in the stunning Renaissance and baroque interiors of today's Royal Palace.

Entry to the Castle is through a series of enclosed courtyards. In the first, the changing of the guard takes place hourly in the shadow of huge baroque sculptures of battling Titans. The entrance to the second courtyard is through the Matthias Gate, which dates from 1614. Directly opposite is the 19th-century Chapel of the Cross. On the other side of the courtyard, the Picture Gallery of Prague Castle contains paintings from the Imperial collections, including minor works by Titian, Tintoretto, Veronese and Rubens. The third courtyard is dominated by St Vitus's Cathedral (► 40–41). To the right, the 18th-century facade of the Royal Palace conceals a network of halls and chambers on various levels, dating from the

Romanesque period onwards. The centrepiece is the magnificent Vladislav Hall. To the right are the former offices of the Chancellery of Bohemia, dating from the early 16th century, where, on 23 May 1618, enraged by the Habsburg Emperor's assault on their traditional priveleges, several Protestant noblemen burst into the far room and threw two Catholic governors and a secretary out of the window. The officials survived the fall but the incident, known as the Defenestration of Prague, marked the start of the Thirty Years War. The Diet Hall was designed by the Renaissance architect Bonifaz Wohlmut in 1563 and its walls are hung with portraits of the Habsburgs. The Riders' Staircase leads down to the remains of the Romanesque and Gothic Palaces and an exhibition on the Castle.

The Castle complex's other outstanding monument is St George's Basilica (➤ 113), and a short walk away is an impressive museum and picture gallery at the Lobkowicz Palace (➤ 68). Beyond the cobblestones and cottages of Golden Lane (➤ 129) is the Daliborka Tower, named after a nobleman imprisoned here on suspicion of complicity in a peasants' revolt. In the Mihulka, or Powder Tower, alchemists were once employed to elicit the secret of turning base metals into gold.

➕ 7J ✉ Hradčany, Praha 1 ☎ 224 372 423 🕐 Apr–Oct daily 9–6; Nov–Mar 9–4 👆 Expensive. Castle admission includes most attractions, except the Lobkowicz Palace 🍴 Cafes (£), restaurants (££–£££) 🚃 Pražský hrad ❓ Changing of the guard every hour on the hour at the main gate. Information centre in the third courtyard

6 Staroměstská radnice (Old Town Hall)

www.pis.cz

The star attraction of Prague's most famous landmark is the enchanting Astronomical Clock.

The Old Town Hall is actually a row of houses adapted over the centuries by the council. In 1338 the burghers enlarged the merchant Volflin's house, and the tower and chapel were added in 1381. Neighbouring Kříž House was acquired in 1387. The house of furrier Mikš was added in 1548 and the house At the Cock in the 19th century.

The main attraction is the Astronomical Clock, which gives the time of day, the months and seasons of the year, the signs of the zodiac, the course of the sun and the holidays of the Christian calendar. On the hour, the figure of Death rings a bell and the 12 Apostles appear above. A cock crows and time is up for the Turk, who shakes his head in disbelief; the Miser eyes his bag of gold; and Vanity admires himself in a mirror.

Inside are the council chamber where Bohemian kings were elected, and a chapel with a distinctive oriel window. Climb the clock tower for views across the red rooftops of the city.

🚏 12K ✉ Staroměstské náměstí 1, Staré Město, Praha 1 ☎ 724 911 556 🕐 Mon 11–6, Tue–Sun 9–6 (hall); Mon 11–10, Tue–Sun 9am–11pm (tower); 🎫 Separate tickets available moderate 🍴 Cafes (££), restaurants (£££) nearby Ⓜ Staroměstská 🚊 Staroměstská

7 Šternberský palác (Sternberg Palace)

www.ngprague.cz

The 17th-century baroque palace, built for Count Wenceslas Sternberg from 1698 to 1707, now houses the National Gallery's impressive collection of Old Masters.

The palace is set back from Hradčany Square (➤ 112): access is through the left-hand entrance of the Archbishop's Palace. The exhibition is

arranged chronologically by the artists' country of origin. The gallery's (➤ 59) proudest possession is Albrecht Dürer's *Feast of the Rose Garlands* (1506). Commissioned for the German merchants' church in Venice, the painting was acquired by Emperor Rudolph II because it features one of his ancestors, Maximilian I (shown in the foreground with Pope Julius II). This glorious masterpiece is one of the few from the fabulous collections assembled by Rudolph to have remained in Prague. German painting is also represented by Holbein the Elder and Lucas Cranach, including a charming *Adam and Eve*. There are works by Geertgen tot Sint Jans, Jan Gossaert and the Brueghels. Outstanding among the later work is a portrait by Rembrandt, *Scholar in his Study* (1634), and several paintings by Rubens, including *Martyrdom of St Thomas* (1637–39), which was commissioned for the church in Malá Strana. By comparison, the Italian Renaissance is less well represented, although Andrea della Robbia, Sebastiano del Piombo and Pietro della Francesca all feature in the collection and there are some fine altar panels by the 14th-century Sienese artist, Pietro Lorenzetti. Paintings by artists of the 18th-century Venetian school, including Tiepolo and Canaletto, and two fine Spanish works, El Greco's *Head of Christ* and a portrait by Goya of Don Miguel de Lardizabal, can also be found in the gallery.

✚ 6J ✉ Hradčanské náměstí 15, Hradčany, Praha 1
☎ 233 350 068 🕐 Tue–Sun 10–6 💰 Moderate; free first Wed of the month 🍴 Cafe (££) 🚇 Malostranská
🚌 Pražský hrad

8 Strahovský klášter (Strahov Monastery)

www.strahovskyklaster.cz

Strahovní means 'watching over', and this ancient religious foundation, famous as a centre of learning, has been guarding the western approaches to Hradčany since the 12th century.

Above the baroque gateway is a statue of the founder of the Premonstratensian Order, St Norbert; to the left of the gate is the Church of St Roch, patron saint of plague victims, commissioned by Rudolf II in 1603 after Prague had narrowly escaped an epidemic. It is now used for modern art exhibitions. The twin-towered Abbey Church of the Nativity has a Romanesque core, but its present appearance dates from around 1750, when Anselmo Lurago remodelled the western facade. Mozart played the organ here on two occasions. The vaulted ceiling is sumptuously decorated with cartouches and frescoes by Jiří Neunhertz,

depicting the legend of St Norbert, whose remains were brought here from Magdeburg in 1627 and reburied in the chapel of St Ursula, on the left of the nave.

The library of the Strahov Monastery is more than 800 years old and among the

finest in Europe. The Theological Hall, built between 1671 and 1679 by Giovanni Orsi, has walls lined with elaborately carved bookcases, stacked with precious volumes and manuscripts. The Philosophical Hall dates from 1782 to 1784, and its entire ceiling is covered with a delightful composition entitled *The Spiritual Development of Mankind*, by Franz Maulbertsch. The library contains more than 130,000 volumes, including 2,500 books published before 1500, and 3,000 manuscripts. The oldest book, the 9th-century *Strahov Gospels*, is on show in the entrance.

➕ 5L ✉ Strahovské nádvoří 1/132, Hradčany, Praha 1
☎ 233 107 718 🕐 Library: daily 9–12, 1–5. Closed Christmas and Easter ♿ Moderate 🍴 Restaurant (££)
🚌 Pohořelec

9 Václavské náměstí (Wenceslas Square)

Wenceslas Square really comes alive after dark, when its restaurants, cinemas and nightclubs attract a boisterous crowd.

Prague's most famous thoroughfare is actually an impressive 750m-long (820yd) boulevard, dominated at its upper end by Josef Schulz's neo-Renaissance National Museum (▶ 154). Once the site of a horse market, Wenceslas Square was later a focus for political demonstration. When the Soviet army occupied Prague in August 1968 it was here that the distraught population gathered to protest. Several months later a student, Jan Palach, burned himself to death in front of the National Museum. Following the collapse of the Communist regime in December 1989, Václav Havel and Alexander Dubcek appeared on the balcony of No 36 to greet their ecstatic supporters. Palach and other victims of the regime are commemorated in a small shrine in front of Josef Myslbek's equestrian statue of St Wenceslas.

Wenceslas Square became a showcase for modern Czech architecture when the traditional two- and three-storey baroque houses were demolished in the 19th century. The neo-Renaissance Wiehl House (No 34) was completed in 1896 and is decorated with florid sgraffito and statuary by Mikuláš Aleš. Many of the sumptuous art nouveau interiors in the Europa Hotel (No 25) have survived and are also worth investigating. The functionalist Koruna palác (No 1), a covered shopping arcade with a stunning glass dome dating from 1911, became the model for other passageways linking the square with the neighbouring streets (the Lucerna, just off the square at Štěpánská 61, was built by Václav Havel's grandfather). The former insurance offices on the corner of Jindřišská could well have been the stuff of nightmares for Franz Kafka when he worked here as a clerk from 1906 to 1907.

➕ 13M ✉ Václavské náměstí, Nové Město, Praha 1
Ⓜ Můstek, Muzeum 🚊 Václavské náměstí

10 Veletržní palác (Veletržní Palace)

www.ngprague.cz

The gallery's outstanding collection of modern Czech and European art is housed in a 1920s constructivist palace.

Designed by Oldřich Tyl and Josef Fuchs for the Prague Trade Fair of 1928, the enormous glass-fronted building was described by the famous modernist architect, Le Corbusier, as 'breathtaking'. The priceless French collection runs the gamut of Impressionist and post-Impressionist artists. Among the highlights are *Two Women among the Flowers* by Monet (1875), *Green Rye* by Van Gogh (1889) and one of

Gauguin's Tahiti paintings, *Flight* (1902). Picasso is represented by several contrasting paintings, ranging from an arresting, primitivist *Self Portrait*, dating from 1907, to *Clarinet* (1911), a classic example of analytic Cubism. There are also works by Braque, Chagall, Derain, Vlaminck, Raoul Dufy, Fernand Léger, Albert Marquet and Marie Laurencin. Among the sculptures are works by Rodin, Henri Laurens and an unusual study of a dancer by Degas.

French painting was a major source of inspiration for Czech artists seeking an alternative to the predominant German culture of the late 19th century. Jan Zrzavy, Bohumil Kubišta and Emil Filla all progressed from neo-Impressionism to more abstract styles. Kubišta's *Still Life with Funnel* (1910) was directly influenced by a similar study by Picasso. Other artists producing Cubist works at the time include Filla, Václav Špála and the sculptor Otto Gutfreund. The Czechs' affinity with French art becomes even more noticeable in the inter-war period, when the two countries were closely bound together by political and diplomatic ties. The crowning moment came in 1935, when the founder of the Surrealist movement, André Breton, visited Czechoslovakia at the invitation of the Prague Surrealists, Jindřich Štyrský, Vincenc Makovsky and Toyen (Marie Čermínová). The exhibition concludes with sections on post-war and contemporary art.

✚ 4E ✉ Dukelských hrdinů 47, Holešovice, Praha 7
☎ 224 301 122 🕐 Tue–Sun 10–6 💷 Expensive
🍴 Cafe (£) Ⓜ Vltavská 🚊 Veletržni 🚉 Holešovice

Best things to do

Top museums

City of Prague Museum
Centuries of history in a nutshell, including an impressive model from the 19th century. Prague hasn't changed all that much (➤ 150).

Franz Kafka Museum
A must for Kafka aficionados, recalling the great man's life and work (➤ 111).

Mucha Museum
Paintings, sketches and poster art by Czech art nouveau artist and illustrator Alphonse Mucha (➤ 152).

Museum of Communism
Admittedly kitschy but good primer on recent history (➤ 151).

Museum of Decorative Arts
Applied arts from over the centuries – strong on Cubism, art nouveau and art deco (➤ 144).

National Museum
Stones, bones and everything else a museum can hold (➤ 154).

National Technical Museum
Packed with historic trains, planes and automobiles. Great for children (➤ 120).

Prague Jewish Museum
Not a Holocaust sight but a celebration of seven centuries of Jewish life in this corner of Old Town. Best places to see, ➤ 38–39.

Sternberg Palace
Best picture gallery in the city, displaying European
masters from the 14th to 18th centuries.
Best places to see, ➤ 48–49.

Veletržní Palace
Dazzling modern art by Van Gogh, Schiele,
Klimt and Picasso and their Czech equivalents.
Best places to see, ➤ 54–55.

Great places to have lunch

Café Louvre (£)

Upstairs restaurant (non-smoking room) with views of the art nouveau architecture on Národní.

✉ Národní třída 22, Nové Město ☎ 224 930 949; www.cafelouvre.cz

🚇 Národní třída 🚌 Národní třída or Národní divadlo

Hotel Questenberk (££)

As well as good food, the restaurant of this refined little hotel just below Strahov Monastery provides wonderful views of Hradčany, Malá Strana and the slopes of Petřín Hill.

✉ Uvoz 15, Hradčany ☎ 220 407 600; www.hotelq.cz 🚌 Pohořelec

Kavárna Slavia (£)

Captivating views of the river and Malá Strana make this art deco café-restaurant special.

✉ Smetanovo nábřeží 2, Staré Město ☎ 224 218 493 🚌 Národní divadlo

Klub architektů (£)

A multi-roomed 14th-century cellar restaurant with excellent cooking from a chef who brings a Mediterranean and Asian influence to traditional Czech dishes. Reservations recommended.

✉ Betlémské náměstí 5A, Staré Město ☎ 224 401 214 🚇 Kárlovy lázně

Nebozízek Restaurant (££)

The food is good but the views from the terrace (reached by funicular) are spectacular. Popular, so reserve a table.

✉ Petřínské sady, 411 Malá Strana ☎ 257 315 329; www.nebozizek.cz
🚇 Funicular Nebozízek

Pizzeria Rugantino (£)

Authentic Italian trattoria just off Old Town Square serving salads, pies and pizzas cooked in a wood-fired oven.

✉ Dušní 4, Josefov ☎ 222 318 172; www.rugantino.cz 🚇 Staroměstská
🚇 Staroměstská

Take a picnic in the small park on Žofín Island (near the National Theatre), where there are panoramic views of Prague Castle.

🚇 Národní třída, Nové Město 🚇 Národní divadlo

U Zlaté Studně (£££)

With its private entrance to the Castle gardens, the terrace restaurant of the 'Golden Well' hotel invites you to enjoy gourmet food while savouring an incomparable prospect over Prague.

✉ U Zlaté Studně 166/4, Malá Strana ☎ 257 533 322; www.goldenwell.cz
🚇 Malostranské náměstí

Villa Richter Restaurants (£–£££)

Set just below the Castle, the villa's three terraced restaurants offer a variety of dining options as well as superlative views.

✉ Staré zámecké schody 6, Hradčany ☎ 257 219 079; www.villarichter.cz
🚇 Malostranská 🚇 Malostranská

Best pubs

Ferdinanda (£)

Good beer from an independent brewery just outside
Prague to accompany classic Czech dishes. Very
reasonable prices, given the location just off Wenceslas
Square.

✉ Corner of Politických vězňů/Opletalova, Nové Město ☎ 222 244
302; www.ferdinanda.cz (in Czech) 🚇 Muzeum

Kolkovna (£)

This was the first of several, very successful attempts
by the Pilsner Urquell brewery to provide a more
discriminating public with an updated version of the
old-fashioned Czech pub.

✉ V Kolkovně 8, Josefov ☎ 224 819 701; www.kolkovna.cz
🚇 Staroměstská 🚊 Staroměstská

Novoměský Pivovar (£)

The 'New Town Brewery' is a labyrinthine establishment, serving
up to 400 diners and drinkers, where you can observe the brewing
process at close quarters.

✉ Vodičkova 20, Nové Město ☎ 222 232 448; www.npivovar.cz
🚊 Vodičkova

Pivovarský dům (£)

As well as the usual light and dark varieties, the 'Brewhouse'
offers a range of beers, including cherry, banana and coffee beers,
as well as a monthly special, and encourages diners to choose an
appropriate brew to accompany each course. All brewed on site.

✉ Corner of Ječná and Lípová 15, Nové Město ☎ 296 216 666;
www.gastroinfo.cz/pivodum 🚊 Štěpánská

U Fleků (£)

Playing unashamedly on its centuries-old reputation, this famous
establishment caters efficiently for the visitors crowding in to

enjoy the convivial atmosphere and the tasty black beer brewed on the premises.

✉ Kremencova 11, Nové Město ☎ 224 934 019/20; www.ufleku.cz ⓂNárodní třída or Karlovo náměstí 🚊 Karlovo náměstí

U Kalicha (£–£££)

'The Chalice' was the pub where that prince of military malingerers, Jaroslav Hašek's *Good Soldier Švejk* arranged to meet his mates 'at half-past six after the war', and his admirers have been making their way here ever since. Accordion music, Švejkian souvenirs, and somewhat higher prices than in less famous places.

✉ Na Bojišti 12–14, Nové Město ☎ 224 912 557; www.ukalicha.cz Ⓜ I P Pavlova 🚊 I P Pavlova

U Medvídků (£)

Large and popular beer hall with its own micro-brewery producing a specially strong beer, though most of what is drunk here is famous Budvar, the original and far superior 'Budweiser'.

✉ Na Perštýné 7, Staré Město ☎ 224 211 916; www.umedvidku.cz Ⓜ Národní třída 🚊 Národní třída

U zlatého tygra (£)

Its tables always filled with faithful regulars, this is probably Prague's most renowned pub, serving perfect Pilsner kept in ideal conditions in its deep and ancient cellars.

✉ Husová 17, Staré Město ☎ 221 221 111; www.uzlatehotygra.cz Ⓜ Staroměstská 🚊 Staroměstská

Stunning views

From the giant metronome on Letná Gardens – there used to be a statue of Stalin here (► 107)

Across Malá Strana from the observatory on Petřín Hill (► 122)

Along the Vltava river valley from the ramparts of Vyšehrad (► 158)

Spectacular views of the city from the astronomical tower of the Klementinum (► 90–91)

Across Staré Město from the tower of Staroměstská radnice (Old Town Hall) (➤ 46–47)

From the Belvedere's garden terrace across to the castle walls and the bridges on the Vltava river (➤ 116–117)

Over the city once you have climbed the 287 steps up to the top of St Vitus's Cathedral tower (➤ 40–41)

From Kampa Island to the iconic Charles Bridge (➤ 89) and Staré Město

Look down on the city at your feet from the south-facing terrace of the Starý Královský palác (Old Royal Palace)

From the Prašná brána (Powder Gate) (➤ 156) across the Obecní dům (Municipal House) and along Celetná towards the Old Town

a walk along the Royal Route

This walk follows the processional route taken by the kings and queens of Bohemia at their coronation.

Start at Obecní dům (► 155) and head down Celetná to Staroměstské náměstí.

The leading burghers and dignitaries of the town rode out to welcome their new monarch at the Powder Gate (► 156), before accompanying him past the cheering crowds on Celetná (► 85) to Old Town Square (► 96–97). Here the procession halted to hear professions of loyalty from the rector of the University and the mayor and council in the Old Town Hall (► 46–47).

Cross the square to Malé náměstí and on to Karlova. At the end of Karlova, cross Křižovnická to Křižovnické náměstí (➤ 92–93) and the Charles Bridge (➤ 89).

Today Karlova is a cluttered, twisting street, lined with galleries and souvenir shops, overshadowed by the fortress-like walls of the former Jesuit stronghold, the Klementinum (➤ 90–91). As the procession passed the Church of St Francis, the King was greeted by the Order of the Knights of the Cross with the Red Star (➤ 92–93).

Cross Charles Bridge to the street called Mostecká and follow Malostranské náměstí round onto Nerudova (➤ 120–121). Climb the hill to the Castle.

At the bridge tower on the Lesser Quarter (Malá Strana) side of Charles Bridge, the mayor handed over the keys to the city and the King then continued through Malostranské náměstí (➤ 119) to the tumultuous sound of bells from St Nicholas's Church (➤ 36–37). The processional route ends at the Matthias Gate ceremonial entrance to Prague Castle.

Distance 2.5km (1.5 miles)
Time 1.5 hours without stops
Start point Obecní dům ☒ Náměstí Republiky, Nové Město ✚ 14K
End point Pražský hrad ☒ Hradčany ✚ 7J
Lunch Bohemia Bagel (£) ☒ Lázeňská 19, Malá Strana
☎ 257 218 192

Best palaces

Arcibiskupský palác (Archbishop's Palace)

This luxurious residence is hidden behind an impressive rococo facade. Unfortunately, the palace is closed to the public apart from special occcasions.

✚ 6J ✉ Hradčanské náměstí 16, Hradčany 🕓 Not open to the public
🚌 Pražský hrad

Černínský palác (Černín Palace)

Dominating the Hradčany the upper part of Černín Palace is Prague's largest palace (➤ 110). The baroque building was constructed between 1669 and 1720 and now houses the Czech Republic's Foreign Ministry.

✚ 5K ✉ Loretánské náměstí, Hradčany 🕓 Not open to the public
🚌 Pohořelec

Lobkowiczký palác (Lobkowicz Palace)

The many-branched Lobkowicz clan numbered some of the country's most powerful historical figures and, following restitution of much of the property confiscated by the Communist regime, members of the family once more play an influential role in society. Among the well-displayed treasures in the palace is *Haymaking*, the only one of Pieter Brueghel's paintings of the seasons in private ownership, plus panoramas of London by Canaletto.

✚ 8J ✉ Jirská 3, Hradčany ☎ 774 557 617 🕓 Daily 10:30–6 👋 Expensive
🚇 Malostranská 🚌 Pražský hrad

Palác Goltz-Kinských (Goltz-Kinsky Palace)

With its lovely rococo embellishments, this palace dates from 1765. Franz Kafka lived above the family shop here, and also attended the German grammar school in another part of the building. The palace is currently being adapted to house the national collection of Asian art.

✚ 12K ✉ Staroměstské náměstí, Staré Město 🚇 Staroměstská
🚌 Staroměstská

Pražský Hrad (Prague Castle)

The towering Gothic spires of St Vitus's Cathedral beyond the neoclassical facade of Prague Castle can be seen from wherever you are in the city (➤ 44–45).

➕ 7J ✉ Hradčany 🕐 Castle complex: daily 5am–midnight. Premises: Apr–Oct daily 9–6; Nov–Mar daily 9–4 🚊 Pražský hrad

Schönbornský palác (Schönborn-Colloredo Palace)

This mid-17th-century baroque palace fell into ruin in the 19th century but was repaired in 1917 and converted into apartments. It now houses the American embassy.

➕ 7K ✉ Tržiště 15, Malá Strana 🕐 Not open to the public 🚊 Malostranské náměstí

Schwarzenberský palác (Schwarzenberg Palace)

This spectacular Renaissance palace has a sgraffiti-adorned facade and fine gables. It makes a magnificent home for the National Gallery's fine collection of baroque painting and sculpture.

➕ 7K ✉ Hradčanské náměstí 2, Hradčany ☎ 223 081 713 🕐 Tue–Sun 10–6 💵 Moderate 🚊 Pražský hrad

Šternberský palác (Sternberg Palace)

The Sternberg Palace houses the National Gallery's collection of European masters (➤ 48–49), including works by Rembrandt, Rubens and Canaletto.

➕ 6J ✉ Hradčanské náměstí 15, Hradčany 🕐 Tue–Sun 10–6 🚊 Pražský hrad

Valdštejnský palác (Wallenstein Palace)

This baroque palace (➤ 126–127) is home to the upper house of the parliament of the Czech Republic (the Senate) and known for its fine gardens.

➕ 9J ✉ Valdštejnské náměstí 4, Malá Strana ☎ 257 071 111 🕐 Sat–Sun 10–4 💵 Free Ⓜ Malostranská 🚊 Malostranské náměstí

Best churches

Betlémská kaple (Bethlehem Chapel)
The twin gables of the Bethlehem Chapel
(► 84–85) draw you to where Jan Hus preached in
the 1400s. The chapel was rebuilt in the 1950s
after being destroyed in the 18th century.
🕇 11L ✉ Betlémské náměstí 4, Staré Město 🕓 Apr–Oct
daily 10–6:30; Nov–Mar Tue–Sun 10–5:30

Chrám svatého Mikuláše
(St. Nicholas's Church)
Best places to see, ► 36–37.

Katedrála svatého Víta
(St Vitus's Cathedral)
Best places to see, ► 40–41.

Klašter svatého Jiři
(St George's Convent and Basilica)
A fine representation of Romanesque architecture
(► 113).
🕇 8J ✉ Bazilika svatého Jiří 5/33, Hradčany
🕓 Daily 10–6

Kostel Panny Marie před Týnem
(Church of Our Lady Before Týn)
The church's striking, soaring Gothic twin towers
can be seen for miles (► 91).
🕇 13K ✉ Staroměstské náměstí (enter from under the red
address marker 604) 🕓 Tue–Sat 10–1, 3–5 🍴 Cafes and
restaurants nearby

Kostel Panny Marie Vítězné
(Church of Our Lady Victorious)
This 17th-century church became a focal point of

the Counter-Reformation after Czech Protestantism was suppressed in 1621.

In 1628 a small wax effigy of the infant Jesus, 'Bambino di Praga', was given to the church and was thought to have miraculous powers (➤ 114).

✚ 8L ✉ Karmelitská 9, Malá Strana ⏱ Mon–Sat 8:30–7, Sun 8:30–8

Kostel svatého Jakuba (St James's Church)

Built on the site of an ancient Gothic church, the baroque St James's church has wonderful acoustics and many concerts and recitals are performed here (➤ 92).

✚ 13K ✉ Malá Štupartská 6, Staré Město ⏱ Daily 9:30–12, 2–4

Kostel svatého Mikuláše Staré (St Nicholas's Church, Old Town)

St Nicholas's Church, in the Old Town (➤ 137), was once hemmed in on three sides by houses so the twin towered facade has a southerly facing aspect rather than the traditional west-facing one. Excellent concerts.

✚ 12K ✉ Staroměstské náměstí, Staré Město ⏱ Daily 10–4 except during services and concerts

Loretánská kaple (Loreta Shrine)

Best places to see, ➤ 42–43.

Good places to take the children

ACTIVITIES
Paddle boats
Paddle boats are available for rent on Slovanský Island (also called Žofín Island).

✉ Nové Město 🚇 Národní třída 🚊 Národní divadlo

Exhibition Grounds (Výstaviště)
The extensive Exhibition Grounds have an old-fashioned fun-fair, a swimming pool, the Mořský Svět (Seaworld) aquarium and a planetarium that presents several shows daily between 2pm and 5pm.

✉ Výstaviště, Holešovice, Praha 7 ☎ 220 103 111 🚊 Výstaviště

Petřín Hill
Climb the hill and enjoy the views, or take the funicular to the top where there is a Mirror Maze and a mini Eiffel Tower (➤ 122).

✉ Malá Strana 🚊 Újezd

Dětský Ostrov
A lovely, safe enclosed playground on a small island just off the Malá Strana side of the Vltava river.

✉ Entrance on Janáčkovo nábřeží (Jiráskův most), Malá Strana 🚊 Zborovská

Tram rides
Prague's red-and-cream trams are fascinating for younger children; number 22 takes the most scenic route. In summer a veteran tram runs between the castle, city centre and Výstaviště.

MUSEUMS
Muzeum hraček (Toy Museum)
The toy array at this castle museum spans 150 years and includes dolls, model houses, cars, aircraft, paddle steamers and more.

✉ Jiřská 6, Hradčany ☎ 224 372
294 🕐 Daily 9:30–5
Ⓜ Malostranská 🚋 Pražský hrad
or Malostranská

Národní technické muzeum (National Technical Museum)

Due to reopen in late 2010 after several years of thorough refurbishment, the museum has a wonderful collection of vintage cars, old trains, motorcycles and aeroplanes, as well as a simulated coal mine (➤ 120).

✉ Kostelní 42, Holešovice, Praha 7
☎ 220 399 111 🕐 Check for times 🚋 Letenské náměstí

Zoologická zahrada (Prague Zoo)

Terribly affected by the great flood of 2002, this fascinating zoo has been completely renovated and, with nearly 5,000 animals, makes a great day out.

✉ U Trojského zámku 3/120, Troja, Praha 7 ☎ 296 112 111 🕐 Jul–Aug 9–7; Apr–May, Sep–Oct 9–6; Nov–Mar 9–4 Ⓜ Nádraží Holešovice, then bus 112 to Zoologická zahrada

THEATRE
Black Light Theatre

Highly entertaining theatre mixing optical illusions, music and dance (➤ 106).

Národní Divadlo Marionet (National Marionette Theatre)

It's well worth investigating the programme of productions here. The theatre has matinée and evening performances (➤ 146).

Green spaces

Palace gardens below Pražský hrad

There are fountains, arbours and balustrades dotted throughout these terraced gardens, each one bearing the name of an aristocratic family. This is an unusual, if steep, way to and from the Castle.

➕ 7J ✉ Valdštejnská 12, Malá Strana 🕐 Aug daily 10–8; Jun, Jul 10–9; May, Sep 10–7; Apr, Oct 10–6 ✋ Moderate 🚇 Malostranská 🚊 Malostranská

Kampa Island

The 'Venice of Prague', Kampa Island is a lovely green area separated from Malá Strana by a tributary of the Vltava River known as the Devil's Stream.

➕ 10L 🕐 At all times ✋ Free 🚊 Hellichova

Královská zahrada (Royal Gardens)

These beautiful 16th-century gardens are home to the Baroque Riding School, the sgraffitoed Ball-Game Hall and the elegant Belvedere (► 116–117).

🕂 8H 🖂 Královská zahrada, Hradčany 🕓 Aug daily 10–8; Jun, Jul 10–9; May, Sep 10–7; Apr, Oct 10–6 ✋ Free 🏛 Královský letohrádek or Pražský hrad

Petřínské Sady (Petřín Hill)

See page 122.

Valdštejnský palác a sady (Wallenstein Gardens)

See pages 69, 126–127.

Vojanový sady (Vojan Gardens)

Hidden behind high walls, these secluded gardens in the middle of Malá Strana were once part of the Archbishop's Palace and are still evocative of medieval times.

🕂 9J 🖂 U Lužického semináře 17, Malá Strana 🕓 Summer daily 8–7; winter daily 8–5 ✋ Free 🚇 Malostranská 🚊 Malostranská

Vrtbovská zahrada (Vrtba Garden)

This 18th-century baroque garden is dotted with sculptures and has a fine staircase. There are wonderful views across Malá Strana from here.

🕂 8K 🖂 Karmelitská 25, Malá Strana 🕓 Apr–Oct daily 10–6 ✋ Moderate 🚊 Malostranské náměstí

Zahrada na valech (Ramparts Garden)

This charming little park runs the whole length of the castle's south face and is filled with features, including an 18th-century fountain, fine trees, an aviary and several pavilions.

🕂 8J 🖂 Pražský hrad (Prague Castle), Hradčany 🕓 Aug daily 10–8; Jun, Jul 10–9; May, Sep 10–7; Apr, Oct 10–6 ✋ Free 🚇 Malostranská then uphill walk 🚌 Pražský hrad or Malostranská

Best luxury places to stay

Alchymist Grand Hotel and Spa (£££)

There are 20 suites and 26 rooms at this 5-star hotel that range from simply luxurious to absolutely indulgent.

✉ Tržiště 19, Malá Strana ☎ 257 286 011; www.alchymisthotel.com

Aria (£££)

This beautiful hotel has a musical theme with rooms named after musicians and floors labelled in different musical genres.

✉ Tržiště 9, Malá Strana ☎ 225 334 111; www.ariahotel.net

Dům U tři Čápů (£££)

In a quiet corner by the Wallenstein Palace in the heart of Malá Strana, this newly opened boutique hotel ('The Three Storks') melds historic ambience with the ultimate in designer luxury.

✉ Tomášská, Malá Strana ☎ 257 210 779; www.utricapu.cz

Four Seasons Hotel Prague (£££)

The luxurious and elegant Four Seasons is in a fabulous riverside location near Karlův most (Charles Bridge).

✉ Veleslavínová 2a, Staré Město ☎ 221 427 000; www.fourseasons.com/prague

The Iron Gate Hotel (£££)

The Iron Gate offers 43 tastefully furnished suites and studios in a historic building which dates back to the 14th century.

✉ Michalská 19, Staré Město ☎ 225 777 777; www.irongate.cz

Josef (£££)

Designed by top architect Eva Jiřičná, the Josef is a sophisticated hotel popular with movie stars and others who appreciate elegant minimalism. There is an excellent gym and a pretty, private garden.

✉ Rybná 20, Staré Město ☎ 221 700 111; www.hoteljosef.com

Le Palais (£££)

The 4-star Le Palais is a belle époque architectural jewel of a hotel with 72 rooms and suites. Modern luxury and 19th-century refinement are perfectly combined here.

✉ U Zvonařky 1, Vinohrady, Praha 2 ☎ 234 634 611; www.palaishotel.cz

Radisson Blu (SAS) Alcron (£££)

Considered one of Prague's most luxurious hotels, the Alcron has beautifully furnished rooms and sumptuous bathrooms. The 211-room hotel has kept its traditional feel yet has contemporary touches and is just off Václavské náměstí.

✉ Štěpánská 40, Nové Město ☎ 222 820 000; www.prague.radissonsas.com

Romantik Hotel U Raka (£££)

Situated just off the picturesque Nový Svět street, this charming log-walled hotel is in great demand and has only six rooms, so ,book well in advance. The rooms are furnished in the style of a traditional country house and the service is excellent. The terraced patio out the back is sublime.

✉ Černínská 10, Hradčany ☎ 220 511 100; www.romantikhotel-uraka.cz

U Zlaté Studně (£££)

This hotel boasts some of the best views in Prague, starting with the baroque palace gardens just below. Peace and quiet are guaranteed here as the hotel is at the top of a closed, steep lane.

✉ U Zlaté Studně 166/4, Malá Strana ☎ 257 011 213; www.goldenwell.cz

Speciality shops

Artěl Glass

High-end glass and novelty gift shop featuring Artěl's own line of luxury glass made from original Czech designs, as well as funky objects, antique books and jewellery. Highly original gift ideas and great for browsing.

✉ Celetná 29, Staré Město ☎ 224 815 085; www.artelglass.com
🚇 Náměstí Republiky

Bakeshop Praha

The best bakery in town, with excellent sourdough and multigrain breads, as well as muffins, croissants, bagels, cookies and cakes. But this place is much more than a bakery. Delicious soups, salads and sandwiches, plus freshly squeezed juices and coffees are all on offer.

✉ Kozí 1, Staré Město ☎ 222 316 823;
www.bakeshop.cz 🚇 Staroměstská

Big Ben Bookshop

This is the perfect port of call if you've forgotten to pack your holiday reading matter. Only English-language books are on sale here, including information guides to Prague and a large selection of children's books.

✉ Malá Štupartská 5, Staré Město ☎ 224 826 565;
www.bigbenbookshop.com 🚇 Náměstí Republiky

Botanicus

All-natural and organic soaps, shampoos, candles, oils, spices and food items. Features plant products harvested on an organic farm not far from Prague. Great source of unique, well-made gifts.

✉ Týn 3, Staré Město ☎ 234 767 446;
www.botanicus.cz 🚇 Staroměstská

www.bata.cz

The Globe Bookstore and Cafe
This bookstore-cum-cafe is a good source for English-language versions of contemporary classics by writers such as Václav Havel.
✉ Pštrossova 6, Nové Město ☎ 224 934 203 🚇 Národní třída

Granat
Bohemia has long been famous for its fiery red garnet gemstones and this shop and another at Panská 1 offer the best selection.
✉ Dlouhá 30, Staré Město ☎ 222 315 612; www.granat.eu 🚇 Náměstí Republiky

Marionety
High-quality, handmade marionettes and puppets based on classic designs going back to the Middle Ages. Much better than the machine-made puppets on the souvenir stalls on Karlova street.
✉ U Lužického semináře 5, Malá Strana ☎ 602 689 918 🚇 Malostranská

Modernista
Contemporary Czech design as well as impeccable reproductions of classic early 20th-century decorative objects, such as Cubist chairs and ashtrays, are on offer here.
✉ Celetná 12, Staré Město ☎ 224 241 300; www.modernista.cz 🚇 Můstek

Moser
The Czech Republic's leading producer of luxury crystal and stemware. The prices are higher than at souvenir stalls, but this is the genuine article. The showroom must be seen to be believed.
✉ Na příkopě 12, Nové Město ☎ 224 211 293; www.moser-glass.com
🚇 Můstek

Qubus
Quirky design shop featuring furniture, lighting, housewares and various art objects from some of the best young Czech designers.
✉ Rámová 3, Staré Město ☎ 222 313 151; www.qubus.cz 🚇 Staroměstská

Exploring

The view from the Charles Bridge at dusk: in the foreground, a procession of dramatic sculptures recedes into the distance; assembled behind them an extraordinary composition of gilded crosses, tented Gothic towers and baroque domes is silhouetted against the sunset. This is Prague in a nutshell. The city's extraordinary charms lie in the painstaking detail of its architecture – a gabled roof, an ornate railing, a sculpted house sign, a pair of Atlantes supporting a portal, a votive statue ensconced in a niche, a street lamp decorated with dancing maidens. Wherever you turn there is some magic to catch the eye.

This book focuses on Central Prague (Praha 1) which is divided into the following districts: Staré Město (Old Town), Nové Město (New Town), Malá Strana (Lesser Quarter), Josefov (Jewish Quarter) and Hradčany (Castle Quarter). Where reference has been made to anything in the outlying areas (Praha 2–10), the district name and Prague area number are given, eg Holešovice, Praha 7.

Staré Město area

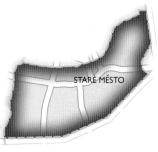

STARÉ MĚSTO

Beyond the Charles Bridge, held within the bend of the River Vltava, is Staré Město (Old Town), historically the most important of the areas that make up this great city. It grew up in the Middle Ages around spacious Staroměstské náměstí (Old Town Square), the ancient marketplace, still a popular meeting place for local inhabitants and visitors alike and one of the most attractive squares in Europe.

To the north of the square are the remains of the Jewish Town, the Josefov (➤ 134), once a medieval labyrinth, now pierced by Prague's prestigious shopping boulevard, Pařížská; to the east, Celetná Street terminates in the imposing gateway of the chisel-capped Powder Gate, the starting point of the Royal Route (➤ 66–67) once traced by monarchs on their way to their coronations. To the west of the square, this ceremonial way passes through Malé náměstí, then along winding Karlova Street towards the river. This part of the Old Town is a maze of narrow streets and arcaded courtyards that conceal churches, gabled houses, aristocratic palaces, brightly painted shopfronts, and earthy pubs cheek by jowl with sophisticated restaurants.

BETLÉMSKÁ KAPLE (BETHLEHEM CHAPEL)

The Bethlehem Chapel (➤ 70) was built by followers of the radical preacher Jan Milíč of Kroměříž between 1391 and 1394. In 1402 Jan Hus was appointed rector and drew huge crowds to his sermons, which were given in Czech, rather than Latin. Hus was a charismatic figure, but his attacks on the wealth and corruption of the Catholic hierarchy did not endear him to his religious superiors.

He eventually overstepped the bounds of orthodoxy, arguing that the Pope had no authority over the Bohemian Church and that doctrine should be based on the scriptures alone. Hus was excommunicated in 1412 and the Bethlehem Chapel was closed. Summoned to defend his teachings at the Council of Constance two years later, Hus consented to leave the safe territory of Prague only after being issued with a guarantee of safe conduct by the Emperor Sigismund. But the Emperor went back on his word: Hus was arrested, condemned as a heretic and, on 6 July 1415, burned at the stake.

Parts of the Chapel were demolished, parts incorporated into the surrounding buildings. Growing enthusiasm for Hus as a national hero, however, eventually led to its reconstruction; perhaps surprisingly, it was the Communist regime, which, in 1949, ordered the work to be begun. The prayer hall is trapezoid in form, the timber roof resting on plain stone supports. The total area measures 798sq m (8,590sq ft) – ample space for the congregations of 3,000 who came to hear Hus speak.

✚ 11L ✉ Betlémské náměstí 4, Staré Město ☎ 224 248 595 ◷ Apr–Oct daily 10–6:30; Nov–Mar Tue–Sun 10–5:30 ✋ Moderate ⊛ Národní třída ⊟ Národní třída or Národní divadlo

CELETNÁ

The street of bakers is one of the oldest in the city and was on the royal processional route. Its handsomely decorated baroque facades conceal in many cases Romanesque or Gothic foundations. An exception is the Cubist House of the Black Madonna (➤ 86). The house at No 36 is the former mint. Some of Prague's best-known restaurants are on Celetná, such as the House At the Golden Vulture (No 22) and At the Spider (No 17). At the Golden Stag (No 11) is now a luxury hotel. Celetná is also a good place to shop for glassware, jewellery and antiques.

✚ 13K ✉ Celetná, Staré Město ✋ Free ⊛ Náměstí Republiky ⊟ Náměstí Republiky

DŮM U ČERNÉ MATKY BOŽÍ (HOUSE OF THE BLACK MADONNA)

While Cubist painting was a Europe-wide phenomenon, Cubist architecture and design were unique to the Czech lands of the Austrian Empire. The movement was short-lived and produced only a small number of buildings, of which this is the most important. Occupying a prominent corner site at the junction of Celetná Street and the Fruit Market (Ovocný trh), it is a striking structure, its facades broken into multiple planes in order to create an unusual interplay of light and shade. The work of the architect Josef Gočár, it was completed in 1912, only months after its neighbour, the elaborately decorated Obecní dům, which seems to belong to another age altogether. Behind a grille on the first floor is the statue of the Madonna that gives the building its name, and which was rescued from the baroque house that once stood here.

The House of the Black Madonna was originally a department store. Nowadays part of its ground floor is occupied by a stylish shop selling reproductions of classic Cubist furniture and other items, for Czech Cubism had ambitions to influence all spheres of life. Upstairs, the equally stylish cafe, a feature of the original building, has been immaculately restored. In addition there is an exhibition on Czech Cubism from 1910 to 1919, with many of the originals on sale downstairs, plus paintings, sculpture and architectural drawings and models.

➕ 13K ✉ Celetná 34, Staré Město ☎ 224 211 746 🕐 Tue–Sun 10–6 ✋ Moderate 🚇 Náměstí Republiky 🚊 Náměstí Republiky

DŮM U KAMENNÉHO ZVONU
(HOUSE AT THE STONE BELL)

This magnificent Gothic tower with its characteristic hipped roof was built as a palace for King John of Luxembourg around 1340. The sculpted decoration of the west facade was rediscovered in the 1960s, having long been concealed by a rococo facelift. Make sure you don't overlook the stone bell on the corner of the building which gives the house its name. Concerts and exhibitions are held here and visitors can see original Gothic features, including extensive fragments of medieval wall painting. The ceiling beams, delicately painted with floral motifs, date from the reign of Charles IV.

➕ 13K ✉ Staroměstské náměstí 13, Staré Město ☎ 224 827 526
🕐 Tue–Sun 10–6 💶 Inexpensive Ⓜ Staroměstská 🚌 Staroměstská

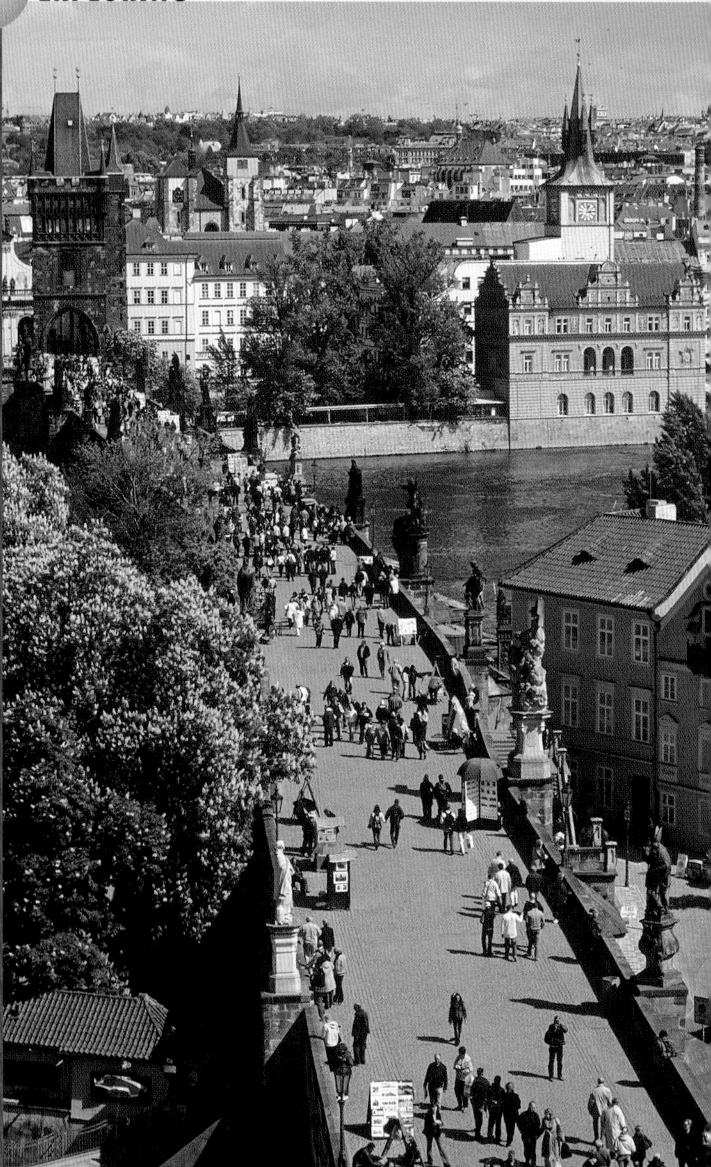

KARLŮV MOST (CHARLES BRIDGE)

Currently undergoing long-term renovation, this remarkable sandstone bridge, designed in 1357 by Petr Parléř for Emperor Charles IV, links the Old Town with the Lesser Quarter. In 1657 a bronze crucifix with a Hebrew inscription was erected on the bridge – the only ornament at that time. The idea caught on and now more than 30 sculptures adorn the parapets. Perhaps the finest of them, by Matthias Braun (1710), shows St Luitgard kissing Christ's wounds in a vision. The figure with the starry halo is St John of Nepomuk, whose tortured body was hurled into the river from this spot in 1393 after he had dared to side with his archbishop against the king. The Old Town Bridge Tower, built in 1391, is also the work of Petr Parléř. The sculptures above the arch show St Vitus and kings Wenceslas IV and Charles IV.

✚ 10K ✉ Karlův most, Staré Město ⏰ Malá Strana Tower: Apr–Sep daily 10–10; Mar, Oct 10–9; Nov–Feb 10–6; Staré Město Tower: Apr–Sep daily 10–11; Mar, Oct 10–10, Nov–Feb 10–8 ✋ Towers: inexpensive

🚇 Staroměstská 🚊 Malostranské náměstí, Staroměstská or Karlovy lázně

KAROLINUM

Founded in 1348 by Charles IV, the Karolinum is the oldest university in Central Europe. It acquired the house of the former mint master, Johlin Rothlev of Kutná Hora, in 1383 (until then classes had been held in churches or private houses). Although Rothlev's house was completely remodelled in the 18th century by František Kaňka, the exquisite oriel window protruding from the facade

on Ovocný trh is a reminder of its medieval origins. The Karolinum's original premises are occupied by the university Rectorate.

✚ 13K ✉ Celetná 13, Staré Město ☎ 224 491 850 🚇 Náměstí Republiky 🚊 Náměstí Republiky

KLEMENTINUM

Once the headquarters of the Jesuit Order in Bohemia, this fortress-like complex enclosed a college, schools, churches, a library, a theatre, an observatory and a printing shop. In 1770 it became part of the university and it is now the home of the

National Library. You need a reader's card for access to the books, but the spectacular Library Hall, one of the city's finest baroque interiors, can be visited in the course of a guided tour. The tour also takes in the equally splendid Mirror Chapel (where concerts are held).

🚇 11K ✉ Klementinum 190, Staré Město ☎ 221 663 111/222 220 879 🕔 Jun–Aug daily 10–8; Apr, Sep 10–6; May 10–7; Nov–Dec 10–4; Jan–Mar, Oct 10–5 ✋ Moderate 🚇 Staroměstská 🚊 Staroměstská

KOSTEL PANNY MARIE PŘED TÝNEM (CHURCH OF OUR LADY BEFORE TÝN)

Most impressive at night when its gaunt, black steeples are eerily lit, Our Lady before Týn is the Old Town parish church (► 70). Although building started in 1380 under the supervision of Petr Parléř, work on the towers was not completed until 1511. For most of that period Týn Church was the stronghold of the Hussite Utraquists, who insisted on taking communion wine as well as bread (the symbolic gilded chalice which hung from the gable was melted down after the Counter-Reformation to make an effigy of the Virgin). The sculpted portal dates from 1390. The interior is a mix of Gothic and baroque styles. Over the high altar are paintings by Karel Škréta, dating from 1640 to 1660, while Gothic features include a pietà and a pewter font (1414). In front of the high altar is the tomb of the Danish astronomer, Tycho Brahe (1546–1601).

🚇 13K ✉ Staroměstské náměstí, Staré Město (enter under the red address marker 604) ☎ 222 322 801 🕔 Tue–Sat 10–1, 3–5 ✋ Free 🚇 Staroměstská 🚊 Staroměstská

KOSTEL SVATÉHO JAKUBA (ST JAMES'S CHURCH)

The Minorite Order of Franciscans commissioned this baroque church in 1689 after its 13th-century predecessor had been destroyed in a fire. The paintings in the nave, galleries and 21 side altars are by a variety of artists, including Franz Voget, Peter Brandl and Václav Reiner, who also contributed the effulgent *Martyrdom of St James* over the high altar. Equally remarkable is the stunning tomb of the Chancellor of Bohemia, Count Vratislav of Mitrovice, on the left-hand side of the nave. It was sculpted in marble and sandstone by Ferdinand Brokoff. A shrivelled arm which dangles just inside the door belonged to a jewel thief caught stealing here in the 16th century.

St James's (➤ 71) is renowned for its musical tradition. A choir sings at high Mass on Sundays, accompanied on the organ, a splendid baroque instrument dating from 1702. There are regular concerts and recitals here.

✚ 13K ✉ Malá Štupartská 6, Staré Město ☎ 224 828 816/7 🕒 Daily 9:30–12, 2–4 🍴 Free Ⓜ Náměstí Republiky 🚊 Náměstí Republiky

KŘIŽOVNICKÉ NÁMĚSTÍ (KNIGHTS OF THE CROSS SQUARE)

Linking the Old Town with the eastern end of Charles Bridge, the square is named after the 13th-century guardians of its predecessor, the Romanesque Judith Bridge, which was destroyed by a great flood in 1342. Despite the constant traffic, this is one of Prague's loveliest squares, dominated by the Old Town Bridge Tower, the Church of St Saviour attached to

the Klementinum (➤ 90–91) and by the knights' own Church of St Francis, its dome thought to have been modelled on St Peter's in Rome. In front of the church, the imposing statue of Emperor Charles IV honours the great ruler as the founder in 1348 of Prague's university. In the basement the Muzeum Karlova Mostů (Charles Bridge Museum) has exhibits relating to the history of the bridge, including a fascinating model of the medieval construction. Also here is a strange subterranean chapel with artificial stalactites and a surviving span of the Judith Bridge.

www.muzeumkarlovamostu.cz

🚼 11L 🖂 Křižovnické náměstí, Staré Město ☎ 776 776 779; 🕓 Museum: May–Sep daily 10–8; Oct–Apr 10–6 👏 Moderate 🚇 Staroměstská
🚌 Staroměstská or Karlovy lázně

MUZEUM BEDŘICHA SMETANY (SMETANA MUSEUM)

The life and work of the 'father of Czech Music', Bedřich Smetana (1824–84), are traced here through letters, documents, scores and musical instruments. Smetana studied piano and composition in Prague, where he heard Liszt and, later, Berlioz perform. A fervent patriot, whose music helped inspire the Czech national revival of the 19th century, he is best known abroad for his emotionally charged symphonic

poem, *Ma vlast (My homeland)* – the famous second movement evokes the swirling currents of the Vltava. He also composed some fine chamber music, as well as numerous operas for the National Theatre, including *The Bartered Bride* and *The Kiss*. Smetana's later life was clouded by personal tragedy: in 1874 he went profoundly deaf after suffering from tinnitus and later lost his reason, dying in an asylum.

➕ 10L ✉ Novotného lávka 1, Staré Město ☎ 222 222 082 ⏱ Wed–Mon 10–12, 12:30–5 ✋ Inexpensive 🚇 Staroměstská 🚊 Staroměstská or Karlovy lázně

STAROMĚSTSKÁ RADNICE

Best places to see, ➤ 46–47.

STAROMĚSTSKÉ NÁMĚSTÍ (OLD TOWN SQUARE)

As early as the 12th century the Old Town Square was a thriving marketplace. Merchants from all over Europe conducted their business here and in the Ungelt (► 98), a courtyard behind the Týn Church. The square was also a place of execution: among the victims were the Hussite rebel Jan Želivský and the 27 Protestant noblemen who died here following the Battle of the White Mountain in 1620 (they are commemorated by white crosses set in the pavement in front of Old Town Hall). Jan Hus, the father of Czech Protestantism, was burned at the stake in Constance, but his monument, a stark sculpture by Ladislav Šaloun (1915), stands in the square.

Today the Old Town Square is full of outdoor cafes, and at Easter and Christmas it is transformed into a marketplace, with wooden huts selling all kinds of small crafts and Czech delicacies. Crowds mill around under the Astronomical Clock on the Old Town Hall (➤ 46–47) as it performs its mesmerizing hourly routine. But the square's chief glory is its architecture: the Renaissance and baroque facades of the houses conceal Gothic substructures and Romanesque cellars. The beautiful rococo embellishments on the Goltz-Kinsky Palace (➤ 68), dating from 1765 (No 12 east side) are by Kilián Dientzenhofer. Directly in front of the Týn Church, the ribbed vaulting in the 14th-century Týn School arcade has survived.

✚ 12K ⊠ Staroměstské náměstí, Staré Město 🚇 Staroměstská
🚊 Staroměstská

STAVOVSKÉ DIVADLO (ESTATES THEATRE)

This famous theatre was built between 1781 and 1783 for Count F A Nostitz-Rieneck, who wanted to raise the cultural profile of the city. On 29 October 1787, the count had his wish when Mozart's opera *Don Giovanni* received its world premiere here after being rejected by the more conservative Viennese theatre managers. 'My Praguers understand me', the composer is reported to have said after conducting the performance from the piano. In 1984 Miloš Forman shot the relevant scenes of his Oscar-winning film *Amadeus* in the auditorium, drawing attention to the need for renovation. That work was completed in the 1990s.

www.narodni-divadlo.cz

✚ 13L ⊠ Ovocný trh 1, Staré Město ☎ 224 901 448 (tickets), 224 901 506 (tours) ✋ Free
🍴 Cafe (££) 🚇 Můstek

UNGELT

From the 12th to the 18th centuries, this courtyard behind the Týn Church was a centre of commerce, where merchants paid *ungelt*, or customs duties. There was also a hostel offering accommodation for travellers here. The complex of 18 buildings

dates from the 16th century onwards and has been restored as shops, hotels and offices. The Granovský palác (Granov Palace), built on the northern side of the square for a wealthy tax collector in 1560, is one of the most distinguished Renaissance buildings in Prague, with sgraffito depicting biblical and classical themes, and a magnificent loggia.

🚩 13K 📧 Týnský dvůr, Staré Město
🍴 Restaurants and cafes in courtyard (££/£££) 🚇 Národní třída 🚌 Národní třída

HOTELS

Betlem Club (££)

The name is a give away – this small hotel is situated just across the street from the Bethlehem Chapel, where the reformer Jan Hus preached in the 15th century. The hotel allows easy access to the Old Town and the bars and restaurants on the square.

✉ Betlémské náměstí 9, Staré Město ☎ 222 221 575; www.betlemclub.cz
🚇 Národní třída 🚊 Karlovy lázně

Černy slon (£££)

A tastefully reconstructed, UNESCO-protected, 14th-century house, only a stone's throw from Old Town Square. The rooms are spacious and furnished with antiques. Bear in mind that there is no lift (elevator).

✉ Týnská 1, Staré Město ☎ 222 321 521; www.hotelcernyslon.cz
🚇 Náměstí Republiky 🚊 Náměstí Republiky

Hotel Paříž (£££)

An eye-catching, neo-Gothic building with art nouveau flourishes, the Paříž has undergone extensive restoration work and is now considered to be one of the city's top hotels.

✉ U Obecního domu 1, Staré Město ☎ 222 195 195; www.hotel-pariz.cz
🚇 Náměstí Republiky 🚊 Náměstí Republiky

Intercontinental (£££)

Built in the 1970s, this was the Communist regime's attempt at a grand hotel to match those in Western capitals. With a fine location by the Čechův Bridge, it offers every comfort of that era, plus the rooftop Zlatá Praha gourmet restaurant.

✉ Pařížská 30, Staré Město ☎ 296 631 111; www.intercontinental.com
🚊 17

The Iron Gate Hotel (£££)

See page 76.

Josef (£££)

See page 77.

RESTAURANTS

Bellevue (£££)
The aptly named Bellevue boasts stunning views of the castle and river. World-class cuisine within a formal, elegant setting. There is a lovely summer terrace and jazz accompanies Sunday lunch.

✉ Smetanovo nábřeží 18, Staré Město ☎ 222 221 443; www.bellevuerestaurant.cz Ⓜ Národní třída 🚊 Karlovy lázně or Národní divadlo

Kavárna Slavia (£)
See page 60.

Klub architektů (£)
See page 61.

Kogo (££)
A buzzing, trendy Italian restaurant with an emphasis on fresh ingredients, serving up delicious favourites.

✉ Havelska 27, Staré Město ☎ 224 214 543; www.kogo.cz Ⓜ Můstek
Also at ✉ Slovanský dům, Na příkopě 22, Nové Město ☎ 221 451 259

La Bodeguita Del Medio (££)
Latin music, pitchers of *mojitos* and Cuban cooking draw the crowds at this busy, stylish restaurant and bar.

✉ Kaprová 5, Staré Město ☎ 224 813 922 Ⓜ Staroměstská
🚊 Staroměstská

La Provence (£££)
From the red leather booths to the silvered mirror over the oak bar, this is the closest you'll get to a real French bistro experience in Prague.

✉ Štupartská 9, Staré Město ☎ 296 826 155; www.kampagroup.com
Ⓜ Náměstí Republiky 🚊 Náměstí Republiky

Lehká Hlava (£)
Casual, cheap and hip vegetarian restaurant with excellent value lunch specials and a regular menu that offers the best of Asian,

Middle Eastern and Mexican cuisines. No smoking throughout.

✉ Boršov 2, Staré Město ☎ 222 220 665; www.lehkahlava.cz

🚇 Staroměstská 🚊 Karlovy lázně or Národní divaldo

Le Terroir (£££)

One of the first Prague restaurants to be awarded a Michelin star, maintaining its reputation as a gourmet's paradise.

✉ Vejvodová 1, Staré Město ☎ 222 220 260; www.leterrior.cz 🚇 Národní třída 🚊 Národní třída

Lokal (£)

A well-established restaurant group has expertly recreated the ambience and food of the old-fashioned Prague pub, but using better ingredients than in the past. Helpful staff will translate the menu.

✉ Dlouhá 33, Staré Město ☎ 222 316 265; www.ambi.cz 🚇 Náměstí Republiky 🚊 Dlouhá třída

Potrefená Husa (£–££)

The 'Shot Goose' is one of a number of designer bar/restaurants pioneered by Prague's big Staropramen brewery. There are beers and wines to accompany the excellent international dishes.

✉ Platnerská 9, Staré Město ☎ 224 813 892 🚇 Staroměstská 🚊 Staroměstská

Rainer Maria Rilke (££)

Meticulously prepared game specialities are a feature of this little privately run establishment, which prides itself on its attentive service and intimate atmosphere.

✉ Karoliny Světlé, Staré Město ☎ 222 221 414; www.rmrikle.cz 🚊 Národní divadlo or Karlovy lázně

Rybí trh (£££)

'The Fish Market' is located in the Ungelt courtyard behind the Týn Church. The freshwater fish, sea fish and shellfish are expensive but worth it, and the wine list is excellent.

✉ Týnský dvůr 5, Staré Město ☎ 224 895 447; www.rybitrh.cz

🚇 Staroměstská or Náměstí Republiky 🚊 Staroměstská or Náměstí Republiky

SHOPPING

ART AND ANTIQUES

Alma Antique

Long-established family firm, a treasure-house of mostly 19th- and 20th-century antiques and collectables, including textiles and toys.

✉ Valentinská 7, Staré Město ☎ 224 813 991 Ⓜ Staroměstská
🚋 Staroměstská

Art Deco Galerie

Delve into this delightful old store, which has an eclectic mix of household items, decorations, clothes and accessories from the 1920s through to the 1960s.

✉ Michalská 21, Staré Město ☎ 224 223 076; www.artdecogalerie-mili.com
Ⓜ Staroměstská 🚋 Staroměstská

Doretheum

The Prague branch of the famous Viennese auction house, with a lavish and tempting display of fine art and antiques, all at fair prices.

✉ Ovjocný trh, Staré Město ☎ 224 222 001 Ⓜ Můstek

Galerie Art Praha

A selection of some of the finest painting and sculpture by Czech and Slovak artists of the 19th and 20th centuries.

✉ Staroměstské náměstí 20, Staré Město ☎ 224 211 087
Ⓜ Staroměstská 🚋 Staroměstská

Galerie České Plastiky

A gallery that focuses mainly on post-1900 Czech sculpture, including statues and busts by the great Otto Gutfreund, Jan Hána and Emanuel Kodet.

✉ Revoluční 20, Nové Město ☎ 222 310 684 Ⓜ Náměstí Republiky
🚋 Náměstí Republiky

Galerie Peithner-Lichtenfels

A small, well-established gallery dealing in works by 19th- and 20th-century Czech masters, including Otto Gutfreund, Bohumil Kubišta, Toyen (Marie Čermínová) and even

Alphonse Mucha, a key figure in the art nouveau movement.

✉ Michalská 12, Staré Město ☎ 224 227 680 Ⓜ Můstek

DEPARTMENT STORES AND SHOPPING MALLS
Kotva

When opened under the Communist regime in 1975, this Swedish-built complex quickly became *the* place to shop. Despite competition from the more glamorous Palladium mall (➤ 162), it is still popular, one reason being Children's Corner, the well-run inside playground where the little ones can be left while you make your purchases.

✉ Náměstí Republiky 8, Staré Město ☎ 224 801 111; www.od-kotva.cz
Ⓜ Náměstí Republiky 🚊 Náměstí Republiky

SOUVENIRS
Blue Praha

A trendy Czech souvenir store selling glassware, artistic T-shirts, hats, fine postcards and other classy mementoes of Prague.

✉ Malé náměstí 14, Staré Město ☎ 224 216 717 Ⓜ Staroměstská

Botanicus

See page 78.

Celetná Crystal

A large store selling a wide range of garnets, amber, porcelain and Bohemian crystal.

✉ Celetná 15, Staré Město ☎ 222 324 022; www.czechcrystal.com
Ⓜ Náměstí Republiky 🚊 Náměstí Republiky

Havelský trh

This daily central fruit and vegetable market also features many souvenir and craft stalls.

✉ Havelská, Staré Město Ⓜ Můstek

Manufaktura

A gift shop with an emphasis on products made from natural materials. A wide range of traditional wooden toys, Christmas ornaments, glassware and handmade soap and cosmetics.

✉ Melantrichova 17, Staré Město ☎ 221 632 480; www.manufaktura.cz

🚇 Můstek

Old Town Square Market

Around the edge of the square, kiosks sell a variety of crafts and souvenirs, including ceramics, wooden toys and wrought-iron work.

✉ Staroměstské náměstí, Staré Město ☎ None 🚇 Staroměstská

🚊 Staroměstská

SPECIALITY SHOPS

Artěl Glass

See page 78.

Bakeshop Praha

See page 78.

Big Ben Bookshop

See page 78.

Futurista Universum

Recently opened and part of the attractive historic building housing the Klub Architektů restaurant (▶ 61), this atmospheric establishment displays superior examples of the skill of contemporary designers.

✉ Betlémské náměstí, Staré Město ☎ 725 128 660; www.futurista.cz

🚇 Národní třída 🚊 Národní třída

Granat

See page 79.

Kubista

On the ground floor of that masterpiece of Czech Cubism, the Black Madonna House, with a stunning but expensive display of superb reproductions of some of the movement's iconic objects.

✉ Ovocný trh 19, Staré Město ☎ 224 236 378; www.kubista.cz

🚇 Národní třída 🚊 Náměstí Republiky

Modernista
See page 79.

Qubus
See page 79.

ENTERTAINMENT

BARS AND PUBS

Bombay Cocktail Bar
This lively cocktail bar is a great place for a few gin and tonics after sampling the tasty north Indian cuisine available in the cellar downstairs.

✉ Dlouhá 13, Staré Město ☎ 222 328 400 🚊 Dlouhá třída

Chateau Rouge
Open until 5am, this bar is often crowded and always lively. The music gets louder as the hours grow later.

✉ Jakubská 2, Staré Město ☎ 222 316 328; www.chapeaurouge.cz
Ⓜ Náměstí Republiky 🚊 Náměstí Republiky

Roxy
This popular club attracts a loyal clientele that appreciates its run-down look and relaxed atmosphere.

✉ Dlouhá 33, Staré Město ☎ 224 826 296; www.roxy.cz Ⓜ Náměstí Republiky 🚊 Dlouhá třída

Tretter's New York Bar
Classic New York-style cocktail bar that's perfect for a quick early evening drink or for a longer, more romantic night out on the town.

✉ V kolkovně 3, Staré Město ☎ 224 811 165; www.tretters.cz
Ⓜ Staroměstská 🚊 Staroměstská

U Medvídků
See page 63.

U Vejvodu
A classic Czech beer hall with efficient waiters and excellent food.

Especially regarded for its high-quality Plzeň beer.

✉ Jilská 4, Staré Město ☎ 224 219 999; www.restauraceuvejvodu.cz

🚇 Národní třída 🚋 Národní třída

U zlatého tygra

See page 63.

CLUBS

La Fabrique

A fun club with tables, a couple of dance floors and a varied crowd of all ages.

✉ Uhelný trh 2, Staré Město ☎ 224 233 137; www.lafabrique.cz

🚇 Národní třída 🚋 Národní třída

Ungelt Jazz & Blues Club

A small club in the 15th-century cellar of a Renaissance building behind Týn Church. A mix of blues, funk and jazz supplied by top Czech performers, with shows every night from 8pm.

✉ Týn 2, Staré Město ☎ 224 895 748; www.jazzungelt.cz

🚇 Náměstí Republiky 🚋 Náměstí Republiky

U Staré Paní

'At the Old Lady' is a sophisticated cellar jazz club that attracts serious names from all over Europe and North America.

✉ Michalská 9, Staré Město ☎ 603 551 680; www.jazzlounge.cz ⏰ Daily 7pm–2am 🚋 Národní třída

BLACK LIGHT THEATRE

Black Light Theatre uses multimedia (film, puppets, music and tricks) together with live actors to create extraordinary effects.

Divadlo Image

✉ Pařížská 4, Staré Město ☎ 222 314 458; www.imagetheatre.cz

🚇 Staroměstská 🚋 Staroměstská

Ta Fantastika

✉ Karlova 8, Staré Město ☎ 222 221 366; www.tafantastika.cz

🚇 Staroměstská 🚋 Staroměstská or Karlovy lázně

BUBENEC

LETNÁ

HRADČANY

MALÁ
STRANA

SMÍCHOV

Hradčany, Malá Strana and beyond

The Hradčany district, on the left bank of the Vltava river, is dominated by Prague Castle, not only a tourist attraction with its cathedral, museums and galleries, but also a seat of government – the Czech president has his offices here. Nowadays, many of the district's mansions and palaces are used as government offices, museums or even restaurants, and monuments in the surrounding areas bear witness to the influence of personalities as diverse as Mozart and Joseph Stalin.

Malá Strana (Lesser Quarter), beneath the castle, is distinguished by the green of its gardens and orchards, created in the 17th century by the aristocrats who built their palaces here. It's much quieter than the Old Town directly across the river. It's also home to many of the city's most pleasant hotels and pensions. Crowning Malostranské náměstí is the majestic, green-domed Church of St Nicholas. Nearer the Vltava, the small neighbourhood of Na Kampě is perfect for an evening stroll.

The area of Smíchov lies to the south, its highlight being the Mozart Museum at Villa Bertramka, at present under restoration.

The districts of Letná, Bubeneč and Holešovice spread out to the north and east, where you'll find an art museum, a giant metronome and a few relics from Prague's Communist past.

BERTRAMKA (MOZART MUSEUM)

This hillside villa, the home of the soprano Josefina Dušek and her composer husband František, was where Wolfgang Amadeus Mozart stayed on his visits to Prague in 1787 and 1791. Although the house was badly damaged by fire in 1873, the rooms Mozart occupied survived. The most highly valued items, apart from the manuscripts, are his harpsichord and a lock of his hair. But his presence can best be felt in the lovely garden. It was here, on the night of 28 October 1787, that Mozart dashed off the sublime overture to his opera, *Don Giovanni*, just one night before the premiere was given in the Estates Theatre (► 97). The museum closed in December 2009 but was reopened with a small exhibition in May 2010 by the Mozart Society with the help of the German Hasse-Gesellschaft and the National Theatre in Prague. Advanced tickets for concerts can be obtained from the society. **www.**mozartovaobec.cz

✚ 17R ✉ Mozartova 169, Smíchov, Praha 5 ☎ 241 493 547 🕐 Check for times 🚌 Bertramka

BÍLÁ HORA (WHITE MOUNTAIN)

In the space of an hour, on 8 November 1620, the Catholic Habsburg army routed the Czech Protestants on this plateau outside Prague, deciding the fate of Bohemia for the next 300 years. The battle is commemorated by a small stone monument and the Church of Our Lady of Victories (1704–14).

Also of interest is the

Renaissance hunting lodge Letohrádek hvĕzda (Star Castle), built between 1555 and 1557 by Ferdinand of Tyrol. In its parkland setting the castle now contains exhibitions devoted to chronicling the work of the writer Alois Jirásek and the painter Mikoláš Aleš.

✚ 5H (off map) ✉ Obora Hvezda 160 00, Liboc, Praha 6 ☎ Castle: 235 357 938 ⏰ Castle: May–Sep Tue–Sun 10–6; Apr, Oct Tue–Sun 10–5 💷 Castle: inexpensive 🚌 Vypich or Petřiny

BŘEVNOVSKÝ KLÁŠTER (BŘEVNOV MONASTERY)

There has been a monastery in Břevnov since AD993, although the present baroque complex, designed by Christoph and Karl Dientzenhofer, dates from 1708 to 1745. After the fall of Communism the monastery was returned to the Benedictines. The remarkable St Margaret's Church, built over a Romanesque crypt, has stunning oval ceiling frescoes by Johann Steinfels, depicting scenes from the legend of St Adalbert, while the Theresian Hall has a magnificent painting of Blessed Günther by Kosmas Assam.

www.brevnov.cz
(Czech/German only)

✚ 5H (off map)
✉ Markétská 28, Břevnov, Praha 6 ☎ 220 406 111
⏰ Guided tour Sat–Sun 10, 2 (also at 4 Apr–Oct)
💷 Inexpensive
🚌 Břevnovský klášter

ČERNÍNSKÝ PALÁC (ČERNÍN PALACE)

So much stone was used in the construction of this vast palace (➤ 68), with a facade stretching the entire length of Loretánské náměstí (135m/443ft), that it was said that the builders were being paid by the cubic metre. Certainly the palace's original owner, Count Jan Černín of Chudenice, Imperial Ambassador to Venice, spared no expense on the interior decoration – the work of the sculptor Matthias Braun and the painter Václav Reiner, among others. In 1948, following the Communist takeover of the government, Jan Masaryk, son of the founder of Czechoslovakia and the only non-Communist member of the government at the time, fell to his death from an upper-floor window into the courtyard below. It has never been determined whether Masaryk jumped or was pushed to his death.

✚ 5K ✉ Loretánské náměstí 5, Hradčany ☎ None ⊙ Not open to the public ▣ Pohořelec

CHRÁM SVATÉHO MIKULÁŠE

Best places to see, ➤ 36–37.

FRANZ KAFKA MUSEUM

Multimedia displays and a unique collection of documents evoke the darkly lit world of Prague's most famous writer (1883–1924). His love-hate relationship with his native city is reflected in his novels *The Trial* and *The Castle*, where, although Prague is never named, its menacing presence looms over its characters. The ambitious museum (▶ 58) draws literary pilgrims from all over the world, though the animated sculpture by David Černý of two men relieving themselves in the courtyard also attracts much attention.

www.kafkamuseum.cz

✚ 10K ✉ Hergetova cihelna, Cihelná 2b, Malá Strana ☎ 221 451 333
🕐 Daily 10–6 Ⓜ Malostranská 🚊 Malostranská

HRADČANSKÉ NÁMĚSTÍ
(HRADČANY SQUARE)

This is a square of stunning Renaissance and baroque facades.
The Archbishop's Palace (No 16) was given its eye-catching rococo
facelift in 1764 by the architect Johan Wirch, and is adorned with
the family crest of Archbishop Antonín Příchovský (➤ 70), home
to the natiional cllection of baroque art. The yellow-fronted
Tuscany Palace (No 5), once owned by the Duke of Tuscany, dates
from 1689 to 1691. Jaroslav Bořita of Martinitz gave his name to
the handsome palace at No 8.

✚ 6J ✉ Hradčanské náměstí, Hradčany 🍴 Café (£) 🚍 Pražský hrad

KATEDRÁLA SVATÉHO VÍTA

Best places to see, ➤ 40–41.

KLÁŠTER SVATÉHO JIŘÍ (ST GEORGE'S CONVENT AND BASILICA)

The burnt-orange basilica and adjoining convent represent the city's best surviving examples of Romanesque architecture, and date from before the first millennium. The basilica's baroque facade, which clashes with the simpler, older Romanesque, was added only in the 17th century.

The large, barn-like interior of the basilica is less busy than neighbouring St Vitus's Cathedral, and for that reason feels more church-like. The church holds the tomb of St Ludmila, Wenceslas's grandmother and Bohemia's first martyr (murdered in 921 on the orders of Wenceslas's mother).

Founded in 973, and rebuilt many times over, the convent was closed down in the late 18th century. It is now the home of the National Gallery's collection of 19th-century Czech art, little known to the outside world but of high quality and great interest.

✚ 8J ✉ Gallery: Bazilika svatého Jiří 5/33, Hradčany ☎ 257 531 644
🕐 Daily 10–6 ✋ Moderate (entry to Basilica included in castle admission)
🍴 Cafe (£), restaurants (££–£££) nearby 🚌 Pražský hrad

KOSTEL PANNY MARIE VÍTĚZNÉ
(CHURCH OF OUR LADY VICTORIOUS)

The chief attraction of this 17th-century church (➤ 70–71) is a wax effigy of the infant Jesus, known by its Italian name 'Il Bambino di Praga'. Believed to have miracle-working properties, the statue was brought from Spain in 1628 by Polyxena of Lobkowicz and presented to the Carmelite nuns.
www.pragjesu.info

✚ 8L ✉ Karmelitská 9, Malá Strana
☎ 257 533 646 🕓 Mon–Sat 8:30–7, Sun 8:30–8 ✋ Free
🚌 Hellichova

KOSTEL SVATÉHO TOMÁŠE
(ST THOMAS'S CHURCH)

This church was established for the Order of the Augustinian hermits by King Wenceslas II, 1285, at the same time as the neighbouring Augustinian monastery, and has undergone many reincarnations over the centuries, the latest between 1723 and 1731 after it was damaged by lightning. The ceiling is covered in frescoes by Václav Reiner depicting the life of St Augustine and, in the dome, the legend of St Thomas. Amazingly, Reiner completed the work in just two years. Other distinguished artists, including Karel Škréta and the sculptor Ferdinand Brokoff, also contributed to the decor, while the paintings (copies) over the high altar, of St Thomas and St Augustine, were commissioned from Rubens (the originals are now in the Šternberský palác ➤ 48–49).

✚ 8K ✉ Josefská 8, Malá Strana ☎ 257 530 556 🕓 Mon–Sat 11:30 –1, Sun 4–6 ✋ Free 🚇 Malostranská 🚌 Malostranské náměstí

KRÁLOVSKÁ ZAHRADA
(ROYAL GARDENS)

These delightful gardens (➤ 116) with wonderful
views were laid out in 1534 in the style of the
Italian Renaissance. Four years later, work began
on the Belvedere, the handsome summer house
presented by Ferdinand I to his wife, Anna
Jagiello. A magnificent arcaded building with a
copper roof resembling an upturned ship's hull, it
was completed in 1564 by Paolo Della Stella, who

also designed the mythological reliefs. The palace is now used for
exhibitions. The sgraffitoed Ball Game Hall towards the western
end of the gardens is the work of the architect Bonifaz Wohlmut,
and was given its name by courtiers who played a form of tennis
here. Tulips grow in the gardens every spring – another reminder

of Ferdinand I, who introduced the flower to Europe from Turkey in the 16th century. Near the western entrance is the Lion's Court, once a menagerie exhibiting bears, panthers, tigers and other beasts.

🕂 8H ✉ Královsky letohrádek, Hradčany ☎ Castle information: 224 372 423 🕐 Gardens: Apr–Oct daily 10–6; (the summer house is open only on special occasions) 🎫 Free 🍴 Restaurant (£££) 🚌 Královský letohrádek or Pražský hrad

LAPIDÁRIUM

Located in an art nouveau pavilion in Výstaviště (the Exhibition Grounds), this is a fascinating review of Czech sculpture from the 11th to the 19th centuries, with explanatory leaflets in English and other languages. One of the earliest exhibits is a beautifully ornamented column from the crypt of the 11th-century Basilica of St Vitus; other displays include the Krocín fountain, a remarkable Renaissance monument which used to stand on Old Town Square, and the 9m-high (30ft) Bear Gate, also known as the Slavata Portal, which once adorned a beautiful baroque garden in the Smíchov district. Ferdinand Brokoff's statues of St Ignatius and St Francis Xavier, now adorning the Charles Bridge, are copies. The originals exhibited here were torn down in the floods of 1890.

🕂 4C ✉ Výstaviště 422, Holešovice, Praha 7 ☎ 233 375 636 🕐 Tue–Sun 12–6 🎫 Inexpensive 🍴 Cafes (£) 🚌 Výstaviště

LENNONOVA ZEĎ' (LENNON WALL)

Opposite the French embassy on Velkopřevorské náměstí, Kampa Island in Malá Strana, this stretch of wall was painted with democratic and pacifist graffiti following John Lennon's death in 1980. A game of cat-and-mouse ensued between police and artists as the wall was continually whitewashed and repainted. After the Velvet Revolution it was allowed to remain, at the request of the French ambassador.

➕ 9L ✉ Velkopřevorské náměstí, Malá Strana 🚌 Hellichova or Malostranské náměstí

LORETA

Best places to see, ➤ 42–43.

MALOSTRANSKÉ NÁMĚSTÍ (LESSER TOWN SQUARE)

The former market square of Malá Strana dates from 1257. Looming over the charming ensemble of baroque buildings is St Nicholas's Church and former Jesuit College (► 36–37). Many of the arcaded houses have now been converted into cafes and restaurants.

The centrepiece of the square is the attractive Renaissance Town Hall (1617–22) on the eastern side. Next door is the house At the Flavins, with a colourful fresco of the Annunciation.

🟩 8K ✉ Malostranské náměstí, Malá Strana 🔲 Malostranská 🚌 Malostranské náměstí

MALTÉZSKÉ NÁMĚSTÍ (MALTESE SQUARE)

This neighbourhood has been associated with the Order of the Knights of Malta since 1169. At the corner of Lázeňská is the former convent of the Order – Maltese crosses can still be seen on the main door and under the roof. Two impressive Gothic towers stand guard over the entrance to the Church of Our Lady Below the Chain, where a painting by Karel Škréta, decorating the main altar, depicts the victory of the Maltese Knights over the Turks at Lepanto in 1571. At the southern end of the square are two grand palaces: the brilliant pink-and-white Palais Turba, now the Japanese Embassy, and the ornate Nostitz Palace (open for chamber music concerts), which houses the Czech Ministry of Culture.

🟩 8L ✉ Maltézské náměstí, Malá Strana 🔲 Hellichova or Malostranské náměstí

119

NÁRODNÍ TECHNICKÉ MUZEUM
(NATIONAL TECHNICAL MUSEUM)

This fascinating museum has undergone complete reconstruction, with the result that its unique collections will be better displayed than ever before, providing evidence of the leading role of Czechs in the advancement of science, technology and industry. The exhibitions are due to be up and running by late 2010. At the heart of the museum is the spacious transport hall, with an array of locomotives and rolling stock, aircraft suspended from the ceiling, and famous makes of cars such as Škoda and Tatra. Simulated streets will offer the chance to see in close-up the development of architectural styles such as art nouveau and Cubism. Among the 40,000 items to be displayed elsewhere in the museum are a variety of film cameras, clocks, astrolabes, sextants, phonographs and much else besides. Working models will be a highlight of the museum, enabling visitors to see at first hand the principals behind the workings of a variety of scientific instruments.

www.ntm.cz

➕ 2F ✉ Kostelní 42, Holešovice, Praha 7 ☎ 220 399 111 🕐 Check locally for times and cost of entry 🚌 Letenské náměstí

NERUDOVA

This street honours Pavel Neruda (1834–91), who was born at No 47 and whose short stories capture perfectly the small-town atmosphere of 19th-century Prague. It's a steep climb to the top – Nerudova was originally called Spur Street after the brake which was applied to coaches on their descent. On your way you will see some wonderful 18th-century house signs (numbers were not

introduced until the 1770s,before which house signs were put above the main door). Look for The Red Eagle (No 6), The Three Fiddles (No 12), The Golden Cup (No 16), The Golden Horseshoe (No 34), The Green Lobster (No 43), the Two Suns (No 47) and The White Swan (No 49). Two magnificent baroque mansions, the Thun-Hohenstein Palace (No 20) and the Morzin Palace (No 5) are now the Italian and Romanian embassies. Nerudova leads eventually to Prague Castle, a wonderful vantage point from which to view the city.

✚ 7K ✉ Nerudova, Malá Strana 🚍 Malostranské náměstí

NOVÝ SVĚT (NEW WORLD)

Nový Svět is a country lane of quaint old houses dating back to the 17th century. Look for U zlatého noha (At the Golden Griffin, No 1), where the astronomer Tycho Brahe once lived, and U zlaté hrušky (At the Golden Pear, No 3), now a fancy restaurant.

www.uzlatehrusky.cz

🕂 5J ⊠ Nový Svět, Hradčany 🍴 Restaurant (£££) 🚊 Brusnice

PETŘÍNSKÉ SADY (PETŘÍN HILL)

Petřín Hill, where pagans made sacrifices and monarchs executed their enemies, is today a haven with panoramic views of the city (► 64, 72). Crowning the summit is the baroque Church of St Lawrence; the ceiling fresco here depicts the founding of an earlier church in 991 on the site of a pagan shrine. The 60m-high (197ft) Observation Tower, modelled on the Eiffel Tower in Paris, was built for the Jubilee Exhibition of 1891, along with the Mirror Maze and a diorama depicting a battle between the Czechs and the Swedes for control of the Charles Bridge in 1648. Encircling the hill is the Hunger Wall, built in 1360 by Charles IV to provide employment in a time of famine. Also here is a working observatory, where you can view the stars and planets on clear nights.

🕂 8M ⊠ Petřínské sady, Malá Strana ☎ Tower: 257 320 112 🚻 Tower and Maze: Apr–Sep daily 10–10; Mar, Oct 10–8; Nov, Feb 10–6 🍴 Restaurant (£££) 🚟 Funicular 🚊 Újezd

PRAŽSKÝ HRAD

Best places to see, ► 44–45.

ŠTERNBERSKÝ PALÁC

Best places to see, ► 48–49.

STRAHOVSKÝ KLÁŠTER

Best places to see, ► 50–51.

a walk through the Lesser Quarter

From Malostranská metro station walk around the corner to Valdštejnská street.

At No 12 a courtyard leads to five terraced baroque gardens that run up to Prague Castle. Each of the gardens bears the name of the noble family that once owned it. One ticket gives entry to all five. Return to the street and continue to Valdštejnské náměstí. The palace at No 4 (▶ 126–127) is home to Wallenstein Gardens (Valdštejnská zahrada).

Take Tomášská to Malostranské náměstí. Walk along the east side of the square to Karmelitská.

Before crossing to Malostranské náměstí, stop to admire Dientzenhofer's baroque church, St Thomas's (▶ 114). The square was once the site of a gallows and pillory. Now café tables spill onto the pavement.

Leave the square by Karmelitská and continue past Tržiště to the Church of Our Lady Victorious (▶ 114) which contains the celebrated statue of Il Bambino di Praga.

On the corner of Tržiště you pass the Vrtba Palace (entry at Karmelitská 25), which has a delightful terraced garden, created around 1720.

Cross Karmelitská and turn left down Harantova. Walk north through Maltézské náměstí (▶ 119) and turn right onto Velkopřevorské náměstí, which leads down to the river.

Beyond the Lennon Wall (▶ 118) and the approach to the Vltava is a little bridge crossing the Čertovka (Devil's Stream). On your left is the waterwheel of the Grand Prior's Mill, which, in common with much of the area, belonged to the Order of the Knights of Malta.

Turn right and follow the river to most Legií, where you can catch a tram back to the centre.

Distance 2km (1 mile)
Time 2 hours without stops
Start point 🚇 Malostranská ✚ 9J
End point most Legií ✚ 10M 🚊 Újezd or Národní divadlo
Lunch U Malého Glena (£) ✉ Karmelitská 23, Malá Strana
☎ 257 531 717; www.malyglen.cz

TROJSKÝ ZÁMEK (TROJA CHÂTEAU)

On the far bank of the Vltava beyond Stromovka park, this huge baroque summer palace was begun in 1679 by Count Wenceslas Šternberg to impress the Emperor. The palace itself is modelled on an Italian villa, but after the death of the original architect, responsibility for the project passed into the hands of a Frenchman, Jean-Baptiste Mathey. To honour the architect's intentions, it is necessary to approach the château from the south, where the formal French garden, restored in the 1980s, leads to an elaborate staircase decorated with heroic statues representing the 'gigantomachia' – the epic struggle between the Gods of Olympus and the Titans. The château apartments now house 19th-century Czech paintings. Most of the ceiling paintings are by an Italian artist, Francesco Marchetti, but for the Grand Hall the count turned to the Flemish painter, Abraham Godyn. His frescoes are Šternberg's effusive tribute to his Habsburg masters, whose triumph over the Ottomans at the gates of Vienna is symbolized by a Turk tumbling from the painting.

www.ghmp.cz

➕ 1B (off map) ✉ U Trojského zámku 1, Troja, Praha 7 ☎ 283 851 614 🕓 Apr–Oct Tue–Thu, Sat–Sun 10–7, Fri 1–7 ✋ Moderate 🚌 Bus 112 from Nádraží Holešovice

VALDŠTEJNSKÝ PALÁC A SADY (WALLENSTEIN PALACE AND GARDENS)

The Imperial General, Albrecht of Wallenstein (1583–1634), was a swashbuckling figure who amassed a tremendous fortune before succumbing to a blow from the assassin's axe. High-walled gardens were laid out in front of the palace (► 69) by Niccolo Sebregondi between 1624 and 1630. The ceiling of the triple-arched *sala terrena*, designed in the Italian Renaissance style by

Giovanni Pieronni, is decorated with scenes from the Trojan Wars. An avenue of bronze sculptures by Adrian de Vries leads from the pavilion (these are copies: the originals were taken by the Swedes during the Thirty Years War). At the far end of the garden is the Riding School, now an exhibition hall.

www.senat.cz

➕ 9J ✉ Valdštejnské náměstí 4, Malá Strana ☎ 257 071 111 🄌 Palace: Sat–Sun 10–5. Gardens: Apr–Oct Mon–Fri 7:30–6, Sat–Sun 10–6 👆 Free
Ⓜ Malostranská 🚌 Malostranská or Malostranské náměstí

VELETRŽNÍ PALÁC
Best places to see, ➤ 54–55.

VÝSTAVIŠTĚ – MOŘSKÝ SVĚT (EXHIBITION GROUNDS – SEAWORLD)

The Exhibition Grounds in Stromovka Park dates from 1891 and has splendid art nouveau pavilions (➤ 117). Here also is Seaworld, devoted to the life of the deep. There are 50 tanks, containing more than 150 species of salt- and freshwater fish from all over the world and a huge coral cave, constructed in 2003. State-of-the-art technology replicates the natural environment with sensitized lighting, while microprocessor-driven water pumps simulate tides.

www.morsky-svet.cz

✚ 3C ✉ Výstaviště 422, Holešovice, Praha 7 ☎ 220 103 275 🚊 Výstaviště

ZLATÁ ULIČKA (GOLDEN LANE)

This row of colourful cottages, built against the walls of Prague Castle, originally provided homes for the archers of the Castle Guard. During the 17th century the palace goldsmiths moved into the area, giving the street its present name. Golden Lane fell into decline and was little better than a slum when Franz Kafka was living with his sister at No 22 during the winter of 1916–17.

✚ 8J ✉ Zlatá ulička, Pražský hrad, Hradčany ⏰ Closed for renovation until mid 2011, otherwise Apr–Oct daily 9–5; Nov–Mar daily 9–4; Rosenberg Palace open while Golden Lane closed ✋ Moderate (entrance included in general castle admission) 🍴 Cafes (£) Ⓜ Malostranská 🚊 Pražský hrad

HOTELS

Alchymist Grand Hotel and Spa (£££)
See page 76.

Aria (£££)
See page 76.

Dům U tři Čápů (£££)
See page 76.

Mandarin Oriental (£££)
In the tranquil heart of Malá Strana, this branch of the luxury hotel chain is a sensitive conversion of an ancient monastery. It offers superlative comfort and service, plus an award-winning spa located in the former chapel.

✉ Nebovidská 1, Malá Strana ☎ 233 088 888; www.mandarinoriental.com
🚍 Hellichova

Romantik Hotel U Raka (£££)
See page 77.

Savoy (£££)
One of Prague's leading hotels, the Savoy is only a stone's throw from Hradčany. The rooms are well appointed and there's a reassuringly unhurried ambience.

✉ Keplerova 6, Hradčany ☎ 224 302 430; www.hotel-savoy.cz
🚍 Pohořelec

Sax (££)
A delightful retro design hotel, with just 22 rooms all devoted to the 1950s, 60s and 70s. Good buffet breakfast, complimentary afternoon tea and free DVD library, plus small spa and sauna.

✉ Jánský vršek 3, Malá Strana ☎ 257 531 268; www.sax.cz
🚍 Malostranské náměstí

U Tří Pštrosů (£££)
Once the centre of a flourishing trade in feathers, 'At the Three

Ostriches' is a charming hostelry next to Charles Bridge, just near Malostranské náměstí. Try to get a room with a view of the bridge.

✉ Dražického náměstí 12, Malá Strana ☎ 257 288 888; www.hotelutripstrosu.cz Ⓜ Malostranská 🚊 Malostranské náměstí

U Zlaté Studně (£££)
See page 77.

RESTAURANTS AND CAFES

Café Savoy (££)
A beautifully restored belle époque cafe from 1893, just off the river, that serves a full breakfast, lunch and dinner menu.

✉ Vítězná 5, Smíchov, Praha 5 ☎ 257 218 192; www.ambi.cz
🚊 Zborovská

Cowboys (££)
Stylish Cowboys is modelled after an American steakhouse, serving a range of charbroiled steaks and fresh fish. The open-air patio tucked under Prague Castle may be one of the loveliest dining areas in the city.

✉ Nerudova 40, Malá Strana ☎ 296 826 107; www.kampagroup.com
🚊 Malostranské náměstí

David (£££)
This quiet and highly regarded restaurant serving reinvented traditional Bohemian dishes gets very busy, so book ahead.

✉ Tržiště 21/611, Malá Strana ☎ 257 533 109; www.restaurant-david.cz
Ⓜ Malostranská 🚊 Malostranské náměstí

Hotel Questenberk (££)
See page 60.

Kampa Park (£££)
Pricey, but worth it for the excellent continental cuisine, river views and occasional celebrity spotting.

✉ Na Kampě 8b, Malá Strana ☎ 296 826 112; www.kampagroup.com
Ⓜ Malostranská 🚊 Malostranské náměstí

Nebozízek Restaurant (££)
See page 61.

Pálffy Palác (£££)
Arguably the most beautiful dining room in Prague, with antique furniture, freshly cut flowers, candles and white linens. In summer you can dine on the terrace just below Prague Castle. The food is continental/international and the chef likes to experiment.

✉ Valdštejnská 14, Malá Strana ☎ 257 530 522; www.palffy.cz
🚇 Malostranská 🚋 Malostranská or Malostranské náměstí

U Maltézských Rytířů (££)
A lovely, old-world restaurant in Malá Strana. Delicious Czech cuisine with the emphasis on game, although salmon and other fish are also on the menu. Reserve a table in advance in the 14th-century Gothic cellar.

✉ Prokopská 10, Malá Strana ☎ 257 530 075; www.umaltezskychrytiru.com
🚋 Malostranské náměstí

U Zlaté Studně (£££)
See page 61.

Villa Richter Restaurants (£–£££)
See page 61.

SHOPPING

SHOPPING MALL
Nový Smíchov
The vast complex called 'New Smíchov' was completed in the heart of the up-and-coming inner suburb of Smíchov in 2001, and, as well as too many shops to count, houses a multiplex cinema, an indoor bowling centre and some two dozen fast-food outlets. You can choose between sushi and burgers and a lot more besides. There is also a children's play area.

✉ Pleňská 8, Smíchov, Praha 5 ☎ 251 101 061; www.novysmichov.eu
🚇 Anděl 🚋 Anděl

SPECIALITY SHOPPING

Galerie Peron
Characterful art gallery with many of the big names of modern
Czech art on its books, as well as a terrace overlooking the Vltava.
✉ U Lužického semináře 12, Malá Strana ☎ 257 533 419; www.peron.cz
🚇 Malostranská náměstí

Marionety
See page 79.

Shakespeare & Sons
Mainly English-language bookshop with thousands of titles, plus
newspapers and an amiably scholarly atmosphere.
✉ U Lužického Semináře 10, Malá Strana ☎ 257 531 894; www.shakes.cz
🚇 Malostranská náměstí

ENTERTAINMENT

CLUBS AND BARS

Bar Bar
This small, friendly cellar bar near the river in Malá Strana is a quirky,
atmospheric place with the art of young Czech and international
artists adorning the walls. Perfect for a drink or first-rate meal.
✉ Všehrdova 17, Malá Strana ☎ 257 312 246; www.bar-bar.cz
🚇 Malostranská 🚇 Újezd

Jazz Dock
This new riverside addition to the city's night-time scene has
already made a name for itself, with the best bands from all around.
✉ Janáčkovo nábřeží 2, Smíchov, Praha 5 ☎ 774 058 838; www.jazzdock.cz
🚇 Arbesovo náměstí

Mecca
Outside the central Prague area, this ultra-cool, multi-level club has
several theme rooms and won the vote for best dance music in
town for several years running.
✉ U průhonu 3, Holešovice, Praha 7 ☎ 283 870 522; www.mecca.cz
🚇 Dělnická

Josefov and beyond

The compact area around the Josefov, the old Jewish quarter, stretches north from Old Town Square to Anežký klášter (St Agnes Convent) with its superb collection of medieval art, and west to the great concert hall of the Rudolfinum. Despite redevelopment at the end of the 19th century, the district retains something of the atmosphere of the ancient ghetto.

JOSEFOV

Sparing only synagogues and other key structures, the rebuilding replaced narrow lanes and alleyways with broad streets and avenues lined with prestigious apartment blocks. Like the Marais in Paris, the Josefov has become an area of high rents, colonized by designer shops, bars and restaurants. The grandest thoroughfare is Pařížská, the city's most exclusive shopping address. More individual shops, as well as interesting hotels, bars and restaurants, are to be found in the surrounding streets.

ANEŽSKÝ KLÁŠTER (ST AGNES CONVENT)

The convent was founded in 1234 by Agnes, sister of King Wenceslas I. St Agnes introduced the Order of Poor Clares into Bohemia and was the first abbess. Completed by the end of the 14th century and sacked by the Hussites in the 15th, the convent was eventually dissolved in 1782. An ambitious restoration programme was completed in the 1990s.

The most impressive building is the Church of the Holy Saviour, an outstanding example of early Gothic architecture. Look for the capitals, which are highly decorated with reliefs showing the rulers of the Přemyslid dynasty. During restoration, the burial place of some of these kings and queens was unearthed, including the tomb of King Wenceslas in the Church of St Francis (which is now used as a concert venue).

The convent houses an exhibition of medieval art from Bohemia and Central Europe (1200–1550). Among the highlights are works by two artists active in the reign of Charles IV: the Master of the Vyšší Brod Altar and Master Theodoric, whose portraits of the saints were intended for the chapel of Karlštejn Castle.

✚ 13H ✉ U milosrdných 17, Josefov ☎ 224 810 628
🕐 Tue–Sun 10–6 💰 Moderate
🚇 Staroměstská, Náměstí Republiky
🚊 Pravnická fakulta or Dlouhá třída

EXPOZICE FRANZE KAFKY
(FRANZ KAFKA EXHIBITION)

A sculpted relief marks the site of the house where
Franz Kafka was born in 1883. Only the doorway of
the original building, At the Tower, remains after a
fire in 1887. A photographic exhibition of Kafka's
life is on the ground floor. A new museum
dedicated to this most influential writer's life and
works (▶ 111) rather overshadows this exhibition,
but it still manages to attract devotees of Prague's
most famous literary figure, particularly as it is his
birthplace.

✚ 12K ⊠ Náměstí Franze Kafky 5,
Staré Město ☎ 222 321 675
🕐 Tue–Fri 10–6, Sat 10–5
✋ Inexpensive 🚇 Staroměstská
🚊 Staroměstská

JEWISH MUSEUM

Best places to see, ▶ 38–39.

KLAUSOVÁ SYNAGOGA
(KLAUSEN SYNAGOGUE)

A number of religious schools and other buildings
known as *klausen* were cleared away after the
great fire of 1689 to make way for this early
baroque synagogue. The fine interior, with barrel-
vaulted roof, stuccoed ceiling ornamentation and
stained-glass windows, has been restored and now
contains an exhibition about local Jewish customs
and traditions, including old Hebrew manuscripts
and prints, beautifully worked Torah ornaments,
skull caps embroidered in satin and velvet, bronze
Hanukkah lamps and a curious wooden alms box

(c1800) with a supplicating hand and arm. The marble Holy Ark, made in 1696 at the expense of Samuel Openheim, has also been restored.

www.jewishmuseum.cz

🚻 11J ✉ U starého hřbitova 3a, Josefov ☎ Jewish Museum: 222 317 191 🕔 Apr–Oct Sun–Fri 9–6; Nov–Mar Sun–Fri 9–4:30. Closed Sat and Jewish hols 💰 Expensive (entry included in admission to Jewish Museum)
🚇 Staroměstská 🚌 Staroměstská or Pravnická fakulta

KOSTEL SVATÉHO MIKULÁŠE (ST NICHOLAS'S CHURCH)

This beautifully proportioned baroque masterpiece was designed by the prolific architect Kilián Dientzenhofer in 1732 and completed three years later. (The sculptures of saints are by Antonín Braun.) St Nicholas (► 71) stands on the site of a much older Gothic church. When, in the spirit of the Enlightenment, the Emperor Joseph II evicted the Benedictines later in the 18th century, on the grounds that they were not performing a useful function, the church was used as a warehouse and fell into disrepair. It was saved during World War I when the commander of the occupying garrison invited local artists to restore Kosmas Asam's frescoes of saints Nicholas and Benedict in the dome. In other respects the building lacks the exuberance of baroque ornamentation.

Since 1920 St Nicholas has belonged to the Czech Reformed (Hussite) Church and is used for concerts; the church has a 2,500-pipe organ.

🚻 12K ✉ Staroměstské náměstí, Staré Město ☎ 224 190 991/2 🕔 Daily 10–4 excluding Mass and concerts 💰 Free 🚇 Staroměstská 🚌 Staroměstská

MAISELOVA SYNAGOGA (MAISEL SYNAGOGUE)

Originally a Renaissance temple, built in 1591 for Mayor Mordechai Maisel, financier to Emperor Rudolph II, the synagogue has a beautifully restored interior, which preserves some of the 16th-century stone carving.

The building now houses an exhibition of sacred religious objects, including items associated with the Torah. This consists of the five books of Moses, handwritten on rolls of parchment by scribes. By tradition the rollers would be elaborately decorated with filials, shields and crowns, superbly wrought in silver or brass and often gilded or encrusted with jewels. Examples of the richly embroidered mantles in which the Torah was wrapped are also on display in the synagogue, along with other items. But the most unusual exhibit is an enormous glass beaker, made between 1783 and 1784 for the Prague Burial Society and painted with a procession of men and women dressed in funereal black.

www.jewishmuseum.cz

🚩 12K ✉ Maiselova 10, Josefov ☎ Jewish Museum: 222 317 191
🕐 Apr–Oct Sun–Fri 9–6; Nov–Mar 9–4:30. Closed Sat and Jewish hols
✋ Expensive (entry included in admission to Jewish Museum)
Ⓜ Staroměstská 🚊 Staroměstská

NÁMĚSTÍ JANA PALACHA (JAN PALACH SQUARE)

'Red Army Square' was renamed after the 1989 Velvet Revolution in honour of Jan Palach, the 21-year-old student who burned himself to death in January 1969 as a protest against the Soviet occupation of Czechoslovakia. The authorities were unmoved but more than 800,000 people joined the funeral procession to Olšanské cemetery, where his remains were laid to rest. On the east side of the square is the philosophy building of Charles University, where Palach attended lectures: on the lower left-hand corner of the facade is a small bronze death mask by Olbran Zoubek.

🚩 11J ✉ Náměstí Jana Palacha, Josefov ✋ Free Ⓜ Staroměstská
🚊 Staroměstská

OBŘADNÍ SÍŇ (CEREMONIAL HALL)

The former Ceremonial Hall of the Prague Burial Society was once used for Jewish burial rites. It now houses a permanent exhibition about Jewish customs and traditions, with particular emphasis on the themes of illness and death.

www.jewishmuseum.cz

✚ 11J ✉ U starého hřbitova, Josefov ☎ Jewish Museum: 222 317 191 ✉ Apr–Oct Sun–Fri 9–6; Nov–Mar 9–4:30. Closed Sat and Jewish hols

🚇 Staroměstská 🖐 Expensive (entry included in admission to Jewish Museum)

🚌 Staroměstská or Pravnická fakulta

PINKASOVA SYNAGOGA (PINKAS SYNAGOGUE)

First mentioned in 1492, this synagogue was founded by Rabbi Pinkas and enlarged in 1535. A women's gallery and council hall were added in the 17th century. Now a Holocaust memorial, its walls have been painstakingly painted with the names of the 77,297 Bohemian and Moravian Jews who perished in Nazi death camps during World War II. (The original lettering was erased by the Communists when they closed the building in 1968, ostensibly to prevent flood damage.) A medieval ritual bath was discovered in the basement during excations, evidence that the site was a Jewish place of worship long before the time of Rabbi Pinkas.

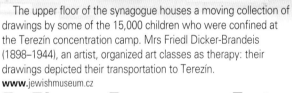

The upper floor of the synagogue houses a moving collection of drawings by some of the 15,000 children who were confined at the Terezín concentration camp. Mrs Friedl Dicker-Brandeis (1898–1944), an artist, organized art classes as therapy: their drawings depicted their transportation to Terezín.
www.jewishmuseum.cz

✚ 11J ✉ Široká 3, Josefov ☎ Jewish Museum: 222 317 191 🕒 Apr–Oct Sun–Fri 9–6; Nov–Mar 9–4:30. Closed Sat and Jewish hols ✋ Expensive (entry included in admission to Jewish Museum) 🚇 Staroměstská 🚋 Staroměstská

RUDOLFINUM

One of Prague's leading cultural venues, the Rudolfinum is also a fine example of neo-Renaissance architecture. During World War II it was used as the German Army HQ and before that (1918–38) it housed the first Czechoslovak parliament. Concert-goers will come to know the Dvořák Hall, home of the Czech Philharmonic Orchestra (chamber concerts and recitals are held in the 'small hall'). The Galerie Rudolfinum is used for art shows and events.
www.ceskafilharmonie.cz

✚ 11J ✉ Náměstí Jana Palacha, Josefov ☎ 227 059 227 🕒 Gallery: Tue–Sun 10–6 ✋ Moderate 🚇 Staroměstská 🚋 Staroměstská

STARONOVÁ SYNAGOGA (OLD-NEW SYNAGOGUE)

Founded around 1270, the Old-New Synagogue is the oldest in Europe that is still open for worship. A typical Gothic building with a double nave, its most unusual feature is the five-ribbed vaulting of the main hall, unique in Bohemian architecture. Other details to look for are the stepped brick gables on the exterior, the grape clusters and vine leaf motifs above the entrance portal, and the medieval furnishings, including stone pews. There are 13th-century Gothic carvings in the tympanum above the Holy

Ark, and the iron lattice enclosing the *almenor* or *bimah* (the tribune from where the Torah is read) dates from the late 15th century. During the sabbath (Saturday) service seven members of the congregation join in the reading. Suspended between two of the pillars is a large red flag embroidered with the Star of David and the traditional Jewish cap. It was presented to the community in 1648 by the Emperor Ferdinand in appreciation of its contribution to the Thirty Years War.

www.jewishmuseum.cz

✚ 12J ✉ Červená 2, Josefov ✪ Apr–Oct Sun–Thu 9–6, Fri 9–5; Nov–Mar Sun–Thu 9–4:30, Fri 9–2. Closed Sat and Jewish hols ✋ Expensive (entry included in admission to Jewish Museum) 🚇 Staroměstská 🚊 Staroměstská

STARÝ ŽIDOVSKÝ HŘBITOV (OLD JEWISH CEMETERY)

One of the oldest Jewish burial grounds in Europe, the Old Jewish Cemetery was founded in the early 15th century: the earliest grave, belonging to Rabbi Avigdor Kara, dates from 1439. There are approximately 12,000 tombstones sprouting obliquely from the earth like broken and decaying teeth. Beneath them lie more than 100,000 bodies, buried layer upon layer in the confined space. The cemetery closed in 1787. This was the last resting place of many prominent members of the Jewish community, including the learned Rabbi Löw (1609), famous as the legendary creator of the Prague Golem. Made from mud from the banks of the Vltava, this monster laboured obediently for his master before he eventually ran amok, causing chaos in the ghetto. The earliest headstones are of sandstone with plain inscriptions, but since the 17th century they have been decorated with marble reliefs indicating the trade or status of the deceased – for example, scissors for a tailor.
www.jewishmuseum.cz

✚ 11J ✉ U starého hřbitova, Josefov ☎ Jewish Museum: 222 317 191
🕐 Apr–Oct Sun–Fri 9–6; Nov–Mar 9–4:30. Closed Sat and Jewish hols
✋ Expensive (entry included in admission to Jewish Museum)
Ⓜ Staroměstská 🚊 Staroměstská

UMĚLECKOPRŮMYSLOVÉ MUZEUM (MUSEUM OF DECORATIVE ARTS)

Once housed in the Rudolfinum, the museum (➤ 58) moved to Josef Schulz's neo-Renaissance building in 1901, and boasts a rich collection of Czech and European applied arts. The collection of Bohemian glass dates back to the Renaissance and is outstanding, as are the Venetian and medieval exhibits. There are selections of Meissen and Sèvres porcelain, exquisite majolica tableware from Urbino and Delft and inlaid cabinets, bureaux and escritoires, from baroque to Biedermeier. The museum shop sells souvenirs.

www.upm.cz

✚ 11J ✉ 17 listopadu 2, Josefov ☎ 251 093 111 ⏰ Tue 10–7, Wed–Sun 10–6 💰 Moderate 🍴 Cafe (£) Ⓜ Staroměstská 🚋 Staroměstská

HOTELS

Hotel Casa Marcello (££)
This small hotel is located in a restored 13th-century building which was once part of St Agnes convent. There is a pleasant terrace and garden in the summer.
✉ Řásnovka 783, Josefov ☎ 222 310 260; www.casa-marcello.cz
🚇 Dlouhá třída

Maximilian (£££)
Not far from the Old Town Square, this plush, Austrian-run boutique hotel, designed by Anglo-Czech arichtect Eva Jiřičná, is on a quiet square facing a church.
✉ Haštalská 14, Josefov ☎ 225 303 111; www.maximilianhotel.com
🚇 Náměstí Republiky 🚇 Dlouhá třída

RESTAURANTS

Amici Miei (£££)
Superior Italian establishment where attentive service complements a range of fine dishes and an extensive cellar. Only the finest of fresh ingredients are used to create such dishes as baked crayfish with courgettes or scampi in filo pastry, followed by pistachio crème brûlée. Every plate is a picture.
✉ Vežeňská 5, Josefov ☎ 224 816 688; www.amicimiei.cz
🚇 Staroměstská 🚇 Staroměstská

Kolkovna (£)
See page 62.

Pizzeria Rugantino (£)
See page 61.

Shelanu Café & Deli (£)
Kosher, New York-style deli near the Old Jewish Cemetery. Ideal for lunch as the menu consists mainly of soups and deli sandwiches. Also serves a full breakfast.
✉ Břehová 8, Josefov ☎ 221 665 141; wwwshelanu.cz 🚇 Staroměstská
🚇 Pravnická fakula

SHOPPING

CLOTHING, JEWELLERY AND ACCESSORIES

Bohème

Specialist in designer Czech knitwear; also sells attractively priced leather goods and interesting accessories.

✉ Dušní 8, Josefov ☎ 224 813 840; www.boheme.cz 🔘 Staroměstská
🚊 Staroměstská or Pravnická fakula

Simpleconceptstore

The concept is that of tempting fashionistas with the latest offerings from a whole range of Parisian big names, with accessories to match.

✉ Pařížská 20, Josefov ☎ 221 773 677; www.simpleconcept.cz
🔘 Staroměstská 🚊 Staroměstská or Pravnická fakula

ENTERTAINMENT

BARS

La Casa Blu

Student-oriented bar with a Latin American theme, serving mostly beer, tequila-based cocktails and Mexican-style bar food. This bar is non-smoking.

✉ Kozí 15, Staré Město ☎ 224 818 270; www.lacasablu.cz
🔘 Staroměstská 🚊 Staroměstská or Pravnická fakula

Tretter's Bar

A classy cocktail lounge graced by glitterati, with a 1930s feel.

✉ V Kolkovně 3, Josefov ☎ 224 811 165; www.tretters.cz 🔘 Staroměstská
🚊 Staroměstská or Pravnická fakula

THEATRES AND CONCERT HALLS

Národní Divadlo Marionet (National Marionette Theatre)

Puppets and costumed actors perform classical operas.

✉ Žatecká 1, Staré Město ☎ 224 819 322; www.mozart.cz 🕐 Performances at 8pm 🔘 Staroměstská 🚊 Staroměstská

Rudolfinum

See page 141.

Nové Město and beyond

The New Town was founded in the 14th century and is now the commercial and administrative heart of the city where new, modern buildings rub shoulders with old. It fills the area from the avenues of Na příkopě and Národní south by the Vltava river down to the dramatic ramparts of Vyšehrad. East of this is Vinohrady, a leafy neighbourhood filled with restaurants and parks.

Even first-time visitors will probably have heard of Wenceslas Square or Václavské náměstí. To call it a square is misleading; it's actually a stately boulevard that is crowned at the top by a massive statue of St Wenceslas on horseback, and the majestic National Museum. Both sides of the 'square' are lined with shops, hotels, cafes and even a casino or two.

The Národní divadlo (National Theatre) and the Café Slavia, once the haunt of dissidents in Communist times, are both highlights of Nové Město and are on the important avenue called Národní třída.

CHRÁM PANNY MARIE SNĚŽNÉ (OUR LADY OF THE SNOWS)

Founded in 1347 by Charles IV, Our Lady of the Snows was to have been the largest church in Prague – 40m (131ft) high and 110m (360ft) long – but the outbreak of the Hussite wars interrupted work on the building. In 1603 the completed choir was restored to the Franciscans and given a baroque facelift and a new vaulted ceiling. All that remains of the 14th-century church are the crumbling pediment over the north gateway and the pewter font. The pretty Franciscan Gardens are now an attractive little public park creating a haven of peace amid the bustle of the city.

🚇 13M ✉ Jungmannovo náměstí 18, Nové Město 🕐 Daily 7–7 except for Mass. Evening concerts: tickets at the door ♿ Free 🚇 Můstek

KOSTEL SVATÉHO CYRILA A METODĚJE (CHURCH OF SAINTS CYRIL AND METHODIUS)

A plaque on the bullet-scarred wall of this Orthodox cathedral commemorates the Free Czechoslovak paratroopers who died here on 18 June 1942, after taking part in the assassination of the Nazi Governor of Bohemia and Moravia, Reinhard Heydrich. Members of the Orthodox community hid the paratroopers in the crypt, but their hiding place was discovered, and after desperate resistance they committed suicide rather than fall into enemy hands. Saints Cyril and Methodius was designated a National Memorial to the victims of the Heydrich Terror.

www.pravoslavnacirkev.cz

🚌 22P 🖂 Resslova 9, Nové Město ☎ 224 916 100 🕙 Mar–Oct Tue–Sun 9–5; Nov–Feb Tue–Sat 9–5 👆 Inexpensive 🚇 Karlovo náměstí 🚊 Karlovo náměstí

MUZEUM ANTONÍNA DVOŘÁKA (DVORAK MUSEUM)

This beautiful baroque mansion, built by Kilián Dientzenhofer between 1717 and 1720 for a prominant Czech nobleman, acquired its present name, Vila Amerika, in the 19th century – there was an eating house of that name nearby. It is therefore entirely appropriate that the building now honours the composer of the 'New World' symphony, Antonín Dvořák (1841–1904). Unfortunately, the palatial interior, with partly restored frescoes by Johann Schlor, is not really suitable for such an intimate exhibition. The exhibits, spread over two floors, include autographed scores, photographs, busts and portraits, correspondence with fellow musicians (the composers Brahms and Tchaikovsky, and the German conductor Hans von Bülow, were among Dvořák's friends and admirers) and a number of personal effects including his viola, Bible and spectacles. The first floor is also used for concerts.

www.nm.cz

🚌 20Q 🖂 Ke Karlovu 20, Nové Město ☎ 224 918 013 🕙 Apr–Sep Tue–Wed, Fri–Sun 10–1:30, 2–5:30, Thu 11–3:30, 4–7; Oct–Mar Tue–Sun 10–1:30, 2–5 👆 Inexpensive 🚇 IP Pavlova 🚊 IP Pavlova or Štěpánská

MUZEUM HLAVNÍHO MĚSTA PRAHY
(CITY OF PRAGUE MUSEUM)

One of the three historic structures that make up the City of Prague Museum (➤ 58) the main building near Florenc Metro station charts the history of the city and includes exhibits which range from the earliest times to the 20th century. Among the various household items on display are slippers, combs and a 14th-century washtub, as well as pottery and coins. The medieval craft guilds are represented in displays of tools, signs and seals, and by some fine examples of their workmanship, including a mural painting of 1406, originally executed for the House at the Golden Angel in Old Town Square. Weapons, model soldiers and cannons and the lock of the original Bethlehem Chapel door (➤ 84–85) are used to illustrate the Hussite period, and there is an impressive collection of statuary, notably a wooden pietà from the

Týn Church (► 91) and a stone Madonna which used to decorate the Oriel Chapel in the Old Town Hall (► 46–47). Another attraction is Antonín Langweil's ambitious model of 19th-century Prague, which can be illuminated to show different areas of the city. It was constructed over a period of 11 years.

www.muzeumprahy.cz

✚ 16J ✉ Na poříčí 52, Karlín, Praha 8 ☎ 224 816 773 🕓 Tue–Sun 9–6 ✋ Inexpensive 🚇 Florenc 🚌 Florenc

MUZEUM KOMUNISMU (MUSEUM OF COMMUNISM)

As a modern visitor to Prague it's all too easy to forget that for more than 40 years (1948–89) what is now the Czech Republic was part of Communist Czechoslovakia, a client state of the Soviet Union. Photographs, household ephemera, agricultural machinery, military hardware, propaganda posters, reproductions of bare food shelves and 'Young Pioneer' classrooms are used to create the exhibition 'Dreams, Reality and Nightmare of Communism'. This portrays an intriguing introduction to life in a satellite Soviet state and a sobering reminder of what the Czech people had to endure. An interrogation room from the 1950s show-trial era is chillingly reproduced, and the persistent ring of a black telephone is a suitably eerie touch.

www.muzeumkomunismu.cz

✚ 13L ✉ Savarin Palace, Na příkopě 10, Nové Město (first floor, same as casino) ☎ 224 212 966 🕓 Daily 9–9 ✋ Moderate 🚇 Můstek

MUZEUM ALPHONSE MUCHA (MUCHA MUSEUM)

This museum (➤ 58) allows you an opportunity to discover the work of one of the great masters of art nouveau, Alphonse Mucha (1860–1939). Mucha began his career in 1887, shortly after studying at the Academy of Arts in Munich, when he found work as a set painter and decorator in Vienna and Paris. His most famous early illustrations were the posters designed for the French actress Sarah Bernhardt. He settled in Prague in 1910, having spent several years teaching.

Other examples of his work can be seen in the Obecní dům, the National Gallery and the Art and Industry Museum. The collection is a representative cross-section of works from the Mucha Foundation: paintings, drawings, lithographs, pastels, sculptures, photographs and personal memorabilia. The museum shop sells a range of souvenirs and gorgeous poster reproductions with the elegant Mucha motif.

www.mucha.cz

🕂 14L 🖂 Panská 7, Nové Město ☎ 221 451 333 🕒 Daily 10–6
🖐 Moderate 🚇 Můstek 🚊 Jindřišská

NA PŘÍKOPĚ (ON THE MOAT)

This busy, pedestrian-only street takes its name from the moat that once formed a boundary between the Old and New Towns. Today it is one of Prague's major shopping thoroughfares, with some compelling architecture from the late 19th century, when a number of major banking houses established their offices here. Particularly impressive is No 18–20. Actually two buildings connected by a bridge, it was designed by Osvald Polívka and completed in 1896. An earlier building, No 10 on the south side, was designed by Kilián Ignac Dienzenhofer in 1743 and served as a casino then as it does now. The colourful mosaics in the lunettes are from cartoons by the Czech artist Mikoláš Aleš.

🕂 13L 🖂 Na příkopě, Nové Město 🖐 Free 🍴 Cafes (£), restaurants (££)
🚇 Můstek, Náměstí Republiky 🚊 Náměstí Republiky

NÁRODNÍ DIVADLO (NATIONAL THEATRE)

Partly funded by public donations, the founding of a National Theatre in this striking building represented the re-emergence of Czech nationalism in the mid-19th century. The foundation stone was laid in 1868, and when the almost completed theatre was destroyed by fire in 1881, more money was raised and a second National Theatre was finished in just two years. The design by Josef Schulz closely followed Josef Zítek's original.

The decoration was entrusted to a group of artists who became known as 'the generation of the National Theatre'. The loggia facing Národní has five arcades decorated with lunette paintings by Josef Tulka, while the attic contains statues by Bohuslav Schnirch, Antonin Wagner and Josef Myslbek. The interior is even more resplendent: in the portrait gallery, Myslbek sculpted bronze busts of Smetana and other contributors to Czech opera and drama, and Mikoláš Aleš, Adolf Liebscher and František Ženíšek filled the foyers with paintings. The stage curtain depicting the story of the National Theatre is by Voitěch Hynais.

Today's performances include theatre, opera and ballet.

www.narodni-divadlo.cz

🕀 11M ✉ Národní 2, Nové Město ☎ Box office: 224 901 448
🍴 Cafe-bar (££) 🚇 Národní třída 🚌 Národní divadlo ❓ Tours Sat–Sun 8:30–11am (tel: 224 902 231)

NÁRODNÍ MUZEUM (NATIONAL MUSEUM)

This stolid neo-Renaissance building, crowned with a gilded dome, dominates Wenceslas Square and houses vast collections of natural history, mineralogy, palaeontology, zoology and anthropology (➤ 58). Badly in need of renovation, the building will be closed for several years from 2011. During this period, selections from its treasures will be on display in the museum's adjoining 'New Building', a hybrid edifice combining the old 1930s stock exchange with the sinister-looking Communist-era Federal Parliament. Its great hall was the scene in 1989–90 of the formal repudiation of one-party rule, presided over by the architect of the 1968 Prague Spring, Alexander Dubček. The building subsequently became the rather unlikely home of Radio Free Europe.

www.nm.cz

🚇 26N ✉ New Building, Vinohradská 1, Nové Město ☎ 224 497 111 🕐 Daily 10–6 ♿ Moderate 🚇 Muzeum 🚌 Muzeum

OBECNÍ DŮM (MUNICIPAL HOUSE)

One of Prague's most engaging art nouveau monuments, Obecní dům was conceived as a community centre with concert halls, assembly rooms, offices and cafes. Antonín Balšánek and Osvald Polívka won a competition for the design and it was completed in 1911. Each of the rooms has its own character, but there is overall unity in the stained-glass windows, inlaid floors, wrought-iron work and walls of polished wood or marble. Scarcely a Czech artist of the period failed to contribute to the interiors. The Smetana Concert Hall was decorated by Karel Špillar and Ladislav Šaloun; Alphonse Mucha was responsible for the Mayor's Salon. Špillar's large mosaic, *Homage to Prague*, on the facade, is also impressive.

www.obecnidum.cz

➕ 14K ✉ Náměstí Republiky 5, Staré Město ☎ 222 002 101 ✋ Tours: moderate 🍴 Cafe (£), restaurants (£££) 🚇 Náměstí Republiky 🚊 Náměstí Republiky ❓ Temporary exhibitions

PAMÁTNÍK 17 LISTOPADU 1989

In an arcade between Wenceslas Square and the National Theatre, at Národní třída 16, is a small plaque commemorating the incident that sparked the Velvet Revolution in 1989. On 17 November a large crowd, made up predominantly of students, headed towards Wenceslas Square from Vyšehrad, where they had been marking the 50th anniversary of the Nazi occupation. When they reached Národní they were confronted by riot police, leaving hundreds severely beaten. Actors and theatre employees immediately called a strike, which led ultimately to the formation of Civic Forum and the fall of the Communist government by the end of that year.

➕ 11M ✉ Národní 16, Nové Město 👋 Free 🚇 Národní třída
🚌 Národní třída

POŠTOVNÍ MUZEUM (POSTAL MUSEUM)

This unusual museum boasts a colourful collection of postage stamps from Czechoslovakia, the Czech Republic and Europe. The backdrop is an exhibition on the history of communications in the region, using prints, old signs and other ephemera. There are also temporary exhibitions. The frescoes in the showroom are by the 19th-century artist Josef Navrátil.

www.cpost.cz

➕ 14H ✉ Nové mlyny 2, Nové Město ☎ 222 312 006 🕓 Tue–Sun 9–12, 1–5 👋 Inexpensive 🚇 Náměstí Republiky 🚌 Dlouhá třída

PRAŠNÁ BRÁNA (POWDER GATE)

Work began on this sturdy Gothic tower in 1475, but was halted eight years later when rioting forced the king to flee the city. It still lacked a roof when Josef Mocker was asked to complete it in the 1870s. The gate acquired its name in the 17th century, when it was used to store gunpowder. It now houses an exhibition on medieval life in Prague.

➕ 14K ✉ Na příkopě, Nové Město 🕓 Daily 10–6 👋 Inexpensive
🚇 Náměstí Republiky 🚌 Náměstí Republiky

VÁCLAVSKÉ NÁMĚSTÍ

Best places to see, ➤ 52–53.

VYŠEHRAD

The twin spires of Vyšehrad church are one of Prague's best-known landmarks. The early history of this settlement is bound in legend surrounding the first dynasty of Czech rulers, the Přemyslids, who established a fortress on the rocky outcrop in the middle of the 10th century.

Though Prague Castle soon began to take precedence, Vyšehrad's value as a stronghold continued to be recognized, and its defences were subsequently strengthened, with ramparts offering superb views over Prague and the valley of the Vltava. From the formidable Brick Gate on the north side of the compound there is access to the mysterious casemates deep within the walls. To the east, beyond the Tábor and Leopold gates, the Romanesque Rotunda of St Martin is a reminder of Vyšehrad's long past, while the Old Deanery stands on the site of an equally ancient basilica.

The Church of St Peter and St Paul has been rebuilt many times; it owes its present neo-Gothic appearance to a 19th-century reconstruction by Josef Mocker. The lawns south of the church make a lovely setting for monumental statues of figures from Czech history and myth. Nearby, an extensive Gothic cellar has fascinating displays on Vyšehrad's history.

Most visitors come to Vyšehrad to pay tribute to the great and good of the Czech nation, whose closely packed and often elaborate tombs fill the Vyšehradský hřbitov (Vyšehrad Cemetery). Among them are those of the composers Dvořák and Smetana, the artist Alphonse Mucha and the writer Karel Čapek.

www.praha-vysehrad.cz

✚ 23T ✉ V pevnosti 159/5b, Vyšehrad, Praha 2 ☎ 241 410 247
🕐 Cemetery: May–Sep 8–7; Mar–Apr, Oct 8–6; Nov–Feb 8–5. Other attractions daily 9:30–6 ✋ Inexpensive 🚇 Vyšehrad 🚊 Vytoň or Albertov

HOTELS

Élite (££)

Restored Renaissance-era town house within easy walking distance of the best restaurants and bars in Nové Město. The coveted suite has original frescoes from the 17th century.

✉ Ostrovní 32, Nové Město ☎ 224 932 250; www.hotelelite.cz
🅜 Národní třída 🚊 Národní třída

Hotel Adria (££)

Hotel Adria is near the Franciscan Gardens and has excellent facilities, including satellite TV, bars and fitness centre.

✉ Václavské náměstí 26, Nové Město ☎ 221 081 111; www.adria.cz
🅜 Můstek 🚊 Václavské náměstí

Hotel Beránek (££)

Housed in a lovely classical building that used to be a bank, this well-maintained hotel has 80 fully equipped modern rooms.

✉ Belehradská 110, Vinohrady, Praha 2 ☎ 221 595 959;
www.hotelberanek.cz 🅜 IP Pavlova 🚊 IP Pavlova

Hotel Pension City (£)

The rooms in this spotless and well-run pension are airy and spacious and a good buffet breakfast is included in the price.

✉ Belgická 10, Vinohrady, Praha 2 ☎ 222 521 606;
www.hotelpensioncity.com 🅜 Náměstí Míru

Pension U Suteru (££)

Tucked away on a quiet street, this spotless 14th-century pension has kept the Gothic architecture in its 10 double/deluxe rooms.

✉ Palackého 4, Nové Město ☎ 233 920 118; www.hotelsprague.cz/usuteru
🅜 Můstek

Yasmin (££–£££)

Probably the largest designer establishment in Prague, with lavish interior landscapes. Just a block away from Wenceslas Square.

✉ Politických vězňů 12 4, Nové Město ☎ 234 100 100 www.hotel-yasmin.cz 🅜 Můstek or Museum 🚊 Václavské náměstí

RESTAURANTS

Aromi (£££)

High-end Italian on a stylish street in Vinohrady. The pasta is home-made and the fish dishes are reputed to be the best in the city. Reserve in advance.

✉ Mánesova 78, Vinohrady, Praha 2 ☎ 222 713 222; www.aromi.cz
🚇 Jiřího z Poděbrad 🚊 Jiřího z Poděbrad

Café Imperial (££)

A classic cafe of the period before World War I, the Imperial has been immaculately restored to its original exuberantly tiled glory.

✉ Na Poříčí 15, Nové Město ☎ 246 011 440; www.hotelimperial.cz
🚇 Náměstí Republiky 🚊 Náměstí Republiky, Masarykovo nádraží or Bíla labut'

Café Louvre (£)

See page 60.

Ferdinanda (£)

See page 62.

Francouzská Restaurace (£££)

The 'French Restaurant' occupies one of most gorgeous interiors of the art nouveau Obecní dům and serves food to match, at a price.

✉ Náměstí Republiky 5, Nové Město ☎ 220 002 770;
www.francouzskarestaurace.cz 🚇 Náměstí Republiky 🚊 Náměstí Republiky

Grossetto (£)

Judging by the queues, it's one of Prague's most popular pizza-pasta restaurants. The secret of its success probably lies in the uniformly generous helpings. Pleasant garden at the rear.

✉ Francouzská 2, Vinohrady, Praha 2 ☎ 224 252 778; www.grosseto.cz
🚇 Náměstí Míru 🚊 Náměstí Míru

Kaaba (£)

A great place to rest from sightseeing, Kaaba has international coffees, teas and newspapers, as well as quality Czech wines.

✉ Mánesova 20, Vinohrady, Praha 2 ☎ 222 254 021 🚇 Muzeum 🚊 Muzeum

Mozaika (££)

Hidden on a tree-lined street, Mozaika is heralded as one of the best places in Prague for a casual meal.

✉ Nitranská 13, Vinohrady, Praha 3 ☎ 224 253 011; www.restaurantmozaika.cz Ⓜ Jiřího z Poděbrad ▣ Jiřího z Poděbrad

Novoměský Pivovar (£)

See page 62.

Pivovarský dům (£)

See page 62.

Pizzeria Kmotra (££)

This Italian cellar restaurant is something of an institution, and offers an extensive choice of wood-fired pizzas.

✉ V Jirchářích 12, Nové Město ☎ 224 934 100; www.kmotra.cz Ⓜ Národní třída ▣ Národní třída or Národní divadlo

Taverna Olympos (££)

A wonderful Greek taverna serving a wide range of national delicacies. Excellent *meze* menu. The large outdoor patio at the back is a treat in the summer. Reserve early.

✉ Kubelíkova 9, Žižkov, Praha 3 ☎ 222 722 239; www.tavernaolympos.cz Ⓜ Jiřího z Poděbrad ▣ Jiřího z Poděbrad

U Kalicha (£–££)

See page 63.

Universal (££)

The atmosphere is cool French bistro but the cooking is more Czech-Mediterranean. Excellent salads, roasted meats and desserts.

✉ V Jirchářích 6, Nové Město ☎ 224934 416 Ⓜ Národní třída ▣ Národní třída or Národní divadlo

Zahrada v Opeře (Opera Garden) (££)

Near the main road that runs across the top of Wenceslas Square, this place has some of the best cooking in the city.

☒ Legerová 75, Vinohrady, Praha 2 ☎ 224 239 685; www.zahradavopere.cz
🚇 Muzeum 🚊 Muzeum

SHOPPING

SHOPPING MALL
Palladium
The biggest and best of several shopping malls opened in recent
years. Lots of shops, a food court, cocktail bars and a dance club.
☒ Náměstí Republiky 1, Nové Město ☎ 225 770 250;
www.palladiumpraha.cz 🚇 Náměstí Republiky 🚊 Náměstí Republiky

SPECIALITY SHOPS
The Globe Bookstore and Café
See page 79.

Knihkupectví Academia
A large bookstore with Czech, German, French and English fiction
and nonfiction, and a large travel section. Have a coffee or a glass
of wine on the second floor.
☒ Václavské náměstí 34, Nové Město ☎ 224 223 511 🚇 Můstek
🚊 Můstek

Moser
See page 79.

Zlatý Křiž
Always crowded with locals at lunchtime, this efficiently run
old-style delicatessen is the place to come for delicious and
inexpensive open sandwiches for your picnic.
☒ Jungmannovo náměstí 19, Nové Město ☎ 222 519 451 🚇 Můstek or
Národní třída 🚊 Národní třída

ENTERTAINMENT

BARS AND CLUBS
Lucerna Music Bar
A two-level underground dance-and-band hall inside the Lucerna
shopping arcade that has great energy and acoustics.

✉ Vodičkova 36, Nové Město ☎ 224 217 108; ww.musicbar.cz 🚇 Můstek
🚊 Můstek

Radost FX
Easily the most famous club in the city. A vegetarian cafe at street
level, a Moroccan-themed lounge in the back, and downstairs a
hedonistic dance club that only gets going after midnight.
✉ Bélehradská 120, Vinohrady, Praha 2 ☎ 224 254 776; www.radostfx.cz
🚇 IP Pavlova 🚊 IP Pavlova

Reduta Jazz Club
One of the oldest jazz clubs in Prague, this is where American
President Bill Clinton jammed with his saxophone in 1994.
✉ Národní 20, Nové Město ☎ 224 933 487; www.redutajazzclub.cz
🚇 Národní třída 🚊 Národní třída

U Fleků
See page 62–63.

THEATRES AND CONCERT HALLS
Laterna Magika (Magic Lantern)
Dramatic performances combining drama, music, light, video and
dance. Performances at 5 and 8pm.
✉ Národní 4, Nové Město ☎ 224 931 482; www.laternamagika.cz
🚇 Národní třída 🚊 Národní divadlo

Smetanova síň (Smetana Hall)
Beautifully restored venue for symphony concerts in the Obecní
dům (Municipal House).
✉ Náměstí Republiky 5, Nové Město ☎ 222 002 101; www.obecnidum.cz
🚇 Náměstí Republiky 🚊 Náměstí Republiky

Státní Opera Praha (State Opera House)
This company performs major Italian, German and Czech operas in
a fine, four-tiered auditorium. Performances usually begin at 7pm.
✉ Wilsonova 4, Nové Město ☎ 224 227 266; www.opera.cz 🚇 Muzeum
🚊 Muzeum

Excursions

There are any number of possible excursions from Prague, many within an hour or two's journey by train or car. The variety of scenery may come as a surprise, from the craggy uplands of Český ráj and the Krkonoše (Giant) Mountains to the woodland slopes of the Berounka Valley. Farther south around Třeboň is a wetland area of lakes and carp-rearing ponds, an ideal habitat for water birds. And there are other surprises in store: a fairy-tale castle on an isolated hilltop, a gloomy limestone cave with dripping stalactites, a charming Renaissance town hall at the centre of a busy market square. The elegant 19th-century resort of Karlovy Vary is famous for its hot mineral springs; Plzeň and České Budějovice are both centres of the brewing industry, and the vineyards of Mělník date back to the reign of Charles IV.

BRNO

The capital of Moravia and the second city of the Republic, Brno is famous for its Motorcycle Grand Prix and trade fairs, but it is also a lively cultural centre with a major university and several theatres (including the Reduta, where Mozart conducted his own compositions in 1767) and some interesting historical sights. Two Brno landmarks – the **Špilberk fortress**, which for centuries served as a Habsburg prison and is now the city museum, and the Gothic Cathedral of St Peter and St Paul – stand on adjacent hills. Below the cathedral is the Old Town. It's worth climbing the tower of the **Old Town Hall** for the views. Notice the middle turret of the hall's Gothic portal, which is askew: according to the local legend, it was left deliberately crooked by the builder as an act of revenge on the burghers for not paying his wages in full.

www.ticbrno.cz

🚩 Radnícká 8 ☎ 542 427 150 🚊 Praha Hlavní nádraží or coach from Praha Florenc ❓ Aug–Sep: International Motorcycling Championship

Špilberk 🕐 May–Sep Tue–Sun 9–6; Oct–Apr Tue– Sun 9–5. **Old Town Hall** ✉ Radnícká 8 🕐 Apr–Sep daily 9–5 💶 Inexpensive for both

a drive around the Bohemian Uplands

Leave Prague, heading northwards on highway 608 to Bohdanovice, then take highway 9 through the village of Libeznice.

Crossing the River Labe, there are views of the vineyards which cluster around the delightful hillltop town of Mělník (➤ 178–179).

Continue on highway 9 to Dubá.

On your way you will pass through Liběchov, which has a château dating from 1730.

Turn left onto the 260 to Úštěk.

The ruins of Hrádek Castle will appear on your left as you approach Úštěk. This charming town possesses an attractive elongated square of Gothic and Renaissance houses, as well as the 'birds' cottages' built like nests on rocky promontories by Italian labourers who constructed the railway in the mid-19th century.

Leave Úštěk on highway 260, travelling northwards. This scenic route crosses the forested Central Bohemian Heights (České středohoří), a designated area of natural beauty. At Malé Březno turn left onto highway 261.

The road now tracks between the River Labe and its sandstone cliffs to the industrial town of Ústí nad Labem. On a promontory south of Ústí you will pass Střekov Castle, with its round Gothic tower. It is said to have been the inspiration for Richard Wagner's opera *Tannhäuser*.

Continue on the 261.

Drive through the orchards and hop gardens of the Labe Valley to Litoměřice, an attractive medieval market town with two town halls (Gothic and Renaissance), as well as numerous baroque churches and town houses.

Cross the river and join highway E55 through Terezín (▶ 182–183) to return to Prague.

Distance 131km (81 miles)
Time 8 hours
Start/end point Střížkov, Praha 9

ČESKÉ BUDĚJOVICE

This sedate old town was founded in 1265 by King Otokar II Přemysl as a base from which to attack his enemies, the unruly Vítkovec clan. During the Hussite Wars the mainly German population remained royalist and stoutly defended the Catholic cause. Commercially, the 16th century was a golden age as České Budějovice exploited its precious silver deposits, but the economic and social dislocation caused by the Thirty Years War put an end to this prosperity and in 1641 the town was ravaged by a terrible fire which damaged or destroyed almost every building of importance. This led to large-scale reconstruction, which accounts for the mainly baroque appearance of today's town. The advent of the railways in the 19th century brought industry to the region and České Budějovice became the third largest city in the country after Prague and Plzeň. Today it is best known for its beer, Budvar.

The town's main square, náměstí Přemysla Otakara II, is one of the largest in Europe: the Town Hall, a graceful building dating from 1727 to 1730, the 13th-century Church of St Nicholas and the lofty Černá Věž (Black Tower) are the main attractions. It's a climb of 360 steps to the Tower's viewing gallery, but well worth it. Visitors who develop a taste for Budvar may like to sign up for a tour of the famous **brewery**.

www.c-budejovice.cz

🛈 Náměstí Přemysla Otakara II 2 ☎ 386 801 413 🚆 Praha Hlavní Nádraží
❓ Aug: International Agricultural Show

Brewery

✉ Karolíny Světlé 4 ☎ 387 705 341 🕔 Daily 9–4, for group tours booked in advance. Daily 2pm, for tours open to the general public 🧑 Moderate

ČESKÝ KRUMLOV

Český Krumlov is simply ravishing. Surrounded by rolling countryside and the wooded Šumava Hills, the old town – a UNESCO World Heritage Site – nestles in a bend of the Vltava

river. For more than 600 years its fortunes were inseparable from those of the aristocratic families residing in the castle: the lords of Krumlov, the Rožmberks, the Eggenbergs and finally the Schwarzenbergs, who were not dispossessed until after World War II. The **castle** is part medieval fortress, part château, magnificently set on a clifftop overlooking the town, and boasting a unique bridge resembling an aqueduct, a picture gallery and the oldest private theatre in Europe. Guided tours include a visit to the Hall of Masks, a ballroom painted in 1748 with *trompe-l'oeil* figures of guests attending a masquerade. The houses of the Latrán, the area around the castle, were originally occupied by servants and court scribes. Buildings here include a 14th-century Minorite Monastery and the Eggenberg Brewery, which still makes its deliveries by horse and cart. Below the castle steps is the medieval former hospice and Church of St Jošt, now converted into private apartments.

The nucleus of the town is on the opposite bank of the Vltava. Prominent on náměstí Svornosti (the main square) is the Town Hall, with attractive arcades and vaulting. Vilém of Rožmberk is buried in the Gothic Church of St Vitus, which dates from 1439. The Latin School, now a music school, and the former Jesuit College, now the Hotel Růže, are also worth a look.

www.ckrumlov.cz

🛈 Náměstí Svornosti 2 ☎ 380 704 622 🚆 Praha Hlavní nádraží (via České Budějovice) ❓ Mid-Jun: Five-Petal Rose Festival; Aug: International Music Festival

Castle 🕐 Apr–May, Sep–Oct Tue–Sun 9–12, 1–4; Jul–Aug Tue–Sun 9–12, 1–5 ✋ Moderate

ČESKÝ ŠTERNBERK

Founded in 1242 on a sheer cliff above the Sázava river, the fortress home of the Šternberk family commands wonderful views of the valley. The castle was remodelled in the baroque style by Italian craftsmen between 1660 and 1670. The rococo Chapel of St Sebastian and the Yellow Room, with an elaborate stucco moulding by Carlo Bentano, are particularly beautiful. There is also a display of silver miniatures and a set of engravings on the staircase which depict scenes from the Thirty Years War.

www.hradceskysternberk.cz

✉ Český Šternberk ☎ 317 855 101 🕐 Jun–Aug Tue–Sun 9–6; May, Sep Tue–Sun 9–5; Apr, Oct Sat–Sun 9–5 ✋ Moderate 🍴 Restaurant (££) 🚌 Bus from Roztyly metro

HRADEC KRÁLOVÉ

Hradec Králové has been the regional capital of Eastern Bohemia since the 10th century. A Hussite stronghold in the 15th century, the town later featured in the Austro-Prussian war of 1866 as the site of the Battle of Königgrätz. At the heart of the old town is an attractive square (actually triangular in shape) known as Žižkovo náměstí after the Hussite warrior, Jan Žižka, who is buried here. Overlooking the square is the 14th-century Cathedral of the Holy Spirit. The free-standing belfry (71.5m/235ft high) is known as the

White Tower, and was added later. Just in front of the tower is a handsome Renaissance town hall. The Jesuit Church of the Assumption, on the southern side of the square, has an attractive 17th-century interior. Two leading art nouveau architects, Osvald Polívka and Jan Kotěra, worked in Hradec Králové. Polívka designed the Gallery of Modern Art, while Kotěra was responsible for the **Regional Museum of East Bohemia** just outside the Old Town.

www.hradeckralove.org

🅘 Gočárova třída 1225 ☎ 495 534 482 🚆 Praha Hlavní nádraží

Regional Museum of East Bohemia

✉ Eliščino nábř 465 ☎ 495 512 391 🕙 Tue–Sun 9–12, 1–6 ✋ Inexpensive

KARLOVY VARY

According to legend, Charles IV was out hunting one day when one of his hounds tumbled into a hot spring and the secret of Karlovy Vary was out. In 1522 Dr Payer of Loket set out the properties of the waters in a medical treatise and their fame spread. By the end of the 16th century there were more than 200 spa buildings, but the present town is mainly 19th century.

There are 12 hot mineral springs in all, housed in five colonnades. The best known (and the hottest) is the Vřídlo, at 72°C (161°F), which spurts to a height of 10m (33ft). The wrought-iron Sadová and the neo-Renaissance Mlýnská colonnades preserve something of their 19th-century atmosphere.

Besides the curative waters, Karlovy Vary is famous for another, more potent liquid: a herb liqueur called *Becherovka* after the chemist who invented the recipe while working at the spa. The area comes alive in summer, when there are concerts and an internationally renowned film festival in early July.

www.karlovyvary.cz

🅘 Mlýnské nábřeží 5 ☎ 355 321 161 🕙 Springs moderate 🚌 Coach from Praha Florenc ❓ May: opening of Spa Season; Jul: International Film Festival

KARLŠTEJN

Perched on a cliff above the Berounka river, Karlštejn was founded by Charles IV in 1348 as a treasury for the imperial regalia and his collection of relics. In the 19th century the fortress was remodelled in neo-Gothic style by Joseph Mocker. Rooms open to the public include the wood-panelled Audience Hall, the Luxembourg Hall and the Church of Our Lady, which has a fine timber ceiling and fragments of 14th-century fresco painting. The magnificent Chapel of the Holy Cross in the Great Tower contains copies of 14th-century panels by Master Theodoric (the originals are in St Agnes Convent in Prague (➤ 135. The walls of the chapel are inlaid with more than 2,000 semiprecious stones.
www.hradkarlstejn.cz

✉ Karlštejn ☎ 311 681 617 🕐 Jul–Aug Tue–Sun 9–6; May, Jun, Sep Tue–Sun 9–5; Apr, Oct Tue–Sun 9–4; Mar Tue–Sun 9–3; Oct–Feb certain days only 9–3 💲 Expensive 🍴 Cafés (£), restaurants (££) nearby 🚉 Karlštejn from Praha-Smíchov ❓ Guided tour only

KONOPIŠTĚ

In 1887 Konopiště Castle was acquired by the heir to the Habsburg throne, Franz Ferdinand, for his Czech wife Sophie Chotek. The Archduke's abiding passion was hunting – in a career spanning 40 years he bagged thousands of animals. Some of the trophies line the walls of the Great Hall. Also worth seeing is Franz Ferdinand's impressive collection of medieval arms and armour and the landscaped garden with peacocks grazing on the lawn. This architypical fairy-tale castle is delightfully set in woodland and is a very popular venue for weddings.

www.zamek-konopiste.cz

✉ Konopiště ☎ 317 721 366 🕐 May–Aug Tue–Sun 9–5; Sep Tue–Sun 9–4; Apr, Oct Tue–Sun 9–4; Nov Sat–Sun 9–3 💲 Expensive 🍴 Restaurant (£) 🚉 Benešov from Praha-Smíchov, then bus ❓ Guided tour only

KŘIVOKLÁT

This beautiful 13th-century castle, with its unusual 35m-high (115ft) round tower, was once the royal hunting lodge of Charles IV. Inside is the vaulted King's Hall, a Gothic chapel with a fine carved altarpiece, a dungeon once used as a prison and now home to a grim assortment of torture instruments, and the Knights' Hall, with a collection of late Gothic paintings and sculptures.

www.krivoklat.cz

✉ Křivoklát ☎ 313 558 440 🕐 Jul–Aug Tue–Sun 9–6; May–Jun, Sep 9–5; Apr 9–4; Oct 10–4 💲 Moderate 🚉 Křivoklát from Praha-Smíchov, change at Beroun ❓ Guided tour only

KUTNÁ HORA

It was the discovery of large deposits of silver and copper ore in the 13th century here which turned Kutná Hora overnight into one of the boom towns of Central Europe. A royal mint, founded at the beginning of the 14th century and known as the **Italian Court**, after Wenceslas II's Florentine advisers, produced its distinctive silver coin, *Pražské groše*, until 1547. Visitors to the Court can see art nouveau frescoes in the Wenceslas Chapel, as well as treasures from the Gothic Town Hall, which burned down in 1770, including a brightly painted wooden statue of Christ, *Ecce Homo* (1502). The **Cathedral of St Barbara** was endowed by the miners and dedicated to their patron saint. Petr Parler's unusual design of three tent-roofed spires supported by a forest of flying buttresses was begun in 1388 but not completed until the end of the 15th century, when Matej Rejšek and Benedikt Reid built the magnificent vaulted ceiling. Behind the **Hrádek museum** (museum of silver) here is a medieval mine where visitors are shown the *trejv*, a horse-drawn winch used for lifting the bags of ore.

   North of Kutná Hora is Sedlec, where, in the 19th century, the Cistercian **ossuary** was turned into a macabre work of art by František Rint, a woodcarver from Ceska Skalice on the Czech–Polish border. There are monstrances, chandeliers and even a Schwarzenberg coat of arms fashioned from human bones.
www.kutnahora.cz

🛈 Palackého náměstí 377 ☎ 327 512 378 🚆 Praha Hlavní nádraží to Sedlec, then bus 🚌 Coach from Praha Florenc bus station ❓ Jun: international guitar competition

Italian Court 🔀 Apr–Sep daily 9–6; Mar, Oct daily 10–5; Nov–Feb daily 10–4
Cathedral 🔀 Apr–Oct daily 9–6; Nov–Mar 10–4
Hrádek museum 🔀 Jul–Aug Tue–Sun 10–6; May–Jun 9–6; Apr, Oct 9–5; Nov Sat–Sun 10–4
Ossuary 🔀 Apr–Sep daily 8–6; Mar, Oct 9–5; Nov–Feb 9–4

LIDICE
In June 1942, following the assassination of the Nazi Governor of Bohemia and Moravia, Reinhard Heydrich, this small village was arbitrarily singled out for reprisal. The men were herded into a farmhouse before being shot, while the women and children were transported to concentration camps and the entire village was razed to the ground. The site is now a shrine with a poignant museum – a wooden cross and a memorial mark the actual place where the men were shot and buried.
www.lidice-memorial.cz
✉ Památník Lidice, 273 54 Lidice ☎ 312 253 063 🔀 Apr–Oct daily 9–6; Mar daily 9–5; Nov–Feb daily 9–4 ✋ Inexpensive 🚌 Bus (Kladno line) from Dejvická or Zličín metro station ❓ 10 Jun: memorial day

LITOMYŠL
This attractive town has one of the largest squares in the Czech Republic, with a Gothic Town Hall and Renaissance and baroque houses. 'At the Knights', built in 1540, has a superb sculpted facade: attend an art exhibition here and take a look at the panelled Renaissance ceiling. The **château** was built between 1568 and 1581. Its exterior is decorated with stunning sgraffiti by Šimon Vlach, and the private theatre is one of the oldest in Europe. Litomyšl is also famous as the birthplace of the composer Bedřich Smetana. His apartment in the château is now a museum, and music festivals take place in his honour throughout the summer.
🚩 Smetanovo náměstí 72 ☎ 461 612 161 🚌 Coach from Praha Florenc bus station ❓ Jun–Jul: Smetana's Litomyšl (opera festival)
Château 🔀 May–Sep Tue–Sun 9–5 ✋ Inexpensive

MĚLNÍK

Perched on a hilltop, with commanding views across the confluence of the Vltava and Labe (Elbe) rivers, is the **château**, Mělník's main tourist attraction. Founded in the 10th century, it originally belonged to the Bohemian royal family and was occupied by several queens, including the wives of John of Luxembourg and Charles IV, who is credited with introducing wine-making to the region. The castle passed into the hands of the Lobkowicz family early in the 17th century and they have owned it intermittently ever since. Mainly of baroque appearance, its northern wing has an impressive Renaissance arcade and loggia with sgraffito decoration, dating from 1555. The rooms have been renovated in a variety of styles; most interesting is the Large Bedroom, which contains an early 17th-century canopied bed with a painting of the Madonna at the head. Visitors are also shown trophies and mementoes belonging to one of the château's more recent owners, Jiří Christian Lobkowicz, a talented racing driver who died tragically on a track in Berlin in 1932. There is a separate

entrance charge for a tour of the 13th-century wine cellars, with tastings. Mělník's grapes are Traminer and Riesling varieties.

You can also tour the Church of St Peter and Paul, built between 1480 and 1520. Its nave is roofed with splendid network and star vaulting and decorated with Renaissance and baroque paintings, including work by Karel Skřeta. The 'pewter' font is actually made of wood. The main draw here is the crypt with its fascinating charnel house, stacked from floor to ceiling with orderly rows of heaped bones – some 15,000 of them at the last count. Some of the skulls are fractured or dented – the result of bullet wounds sustained in the battles of the Thirty Years War.

www.melnik.info

🔒 Náměstí Mirů 11 ☎ 315 627 503 🚌 Coach from Praha Florenc bus station

Château ☎ 315 622 121 🕐 Daily 9:30–6 ✋ Moderate

PLZEŇ

Beer has been brewed in Plzeň since 1295 and the Pilsner Urquell **brewery** is the main attraction in this largely industrial town. The guided tour of the cellars (there are 9km/5.5 miles in all) includes a visit to the extravagantly decorated beer hall, definitely an experience not to be missed. Plzeň's main square, náměstí Republiky, has some fine Renaissance and baroque town houses

and is dominated by the Gothic Cathedral of St Bartholomew, which has the tallest steeple in the country (102m/335ft). Close by is a fascinating **Museum of Brewing** housed, appropriately enough, in a medieval malthouse.

www.plzen-city.cz

🔒 Náměstí Republiky 41 🚆 Praha Hlavní nádraží

Brewery visitor centre 🕐 377 062 888 🕐 Brewery tours in English: daily 12:45, 2.15 and 4pm unless reserved in advance

Museum of Brewing ✉ Veleslavinova 6 ☎ 377 235 574

🕐 10–6 (Jan–Mar 10–5) ✋ Moderate

TÁBOR

In a marvellous location on a bluff commanding the Lužnice Valley, Tábor takes its name from the biblical mountain where Christ is said to have appeared transfigured to his disciples. After the death of Jan Hus, the Hussites transferred their allegiance to the one-eyed general Jan Žižka, who continued the struggle against the Catholics. He encamped here in 1420 and held out successfully for four years until his death in battle. The town's attractive main square, about 20 minutes' walk from the station, is named after him and there is a statue by Josef Strachovksý.

The tower of the Church of the Transfiguration, which dates from the 16th century, offers the best views of the gabled Renaissance and classical houses and of the town itself, which is seen melting into the distance.

An exhibition in the neo-Gothic **Town Hall** presents an excellent account of the Hussite Movement. Don't miss the tour of the labyrinthine tunnels below the ground. Dating from the 15th century, they were used variously as beer cellars, as a prison for unruly women and as an escape route in time of war. When you emerge, you'll find yourself near a cafe where you can sit and relax. The narrow twisting streets of the Old Town are a delight, although you may get lost from time to time. This is no accident – when the town was laid out Žižka's followers wanted to make life as confusing as possible for the enemy.

A pleasant stroll along the banks of the Lužnice river leads to the Bechyně Gate and Kotnov Castle, with its distictive round tower. Inside are some fascinating displays on medieval life in the region, with costumes, archaeological finds, farming implements and weapons. The views from the tower are a bonus.

Only 2km (1 mile) away, across beautiful countryside, is the hamlet of Klokoty, with a baroque convent and church dating from the early 18th century. The wayside shrines along the footpath mark it out as a place of Catholic pilgrimage.

On the other side of town, between Žižkovo and Tržní náměstí, is a Renaissance water tower decorated with vaulted gables and dating from 1497.

The water was pumped to the town's seven fountains from the Jordan, the oldest dam in Europe, via a system of wooden pipes.

www.tabor.cz

ℹ️ Zižkovo náměstí 2 ☎ 381 486 230 🚆 Praha Hlavní nádraží 🛈 Sep: Tábor Meetings, a festival of parades, music and events

Town Hall Museum

✉️ Náměstí Mikuláše z Husi 44 🕐 Apr–Oct daily 8:30–5; Nov–Mar Mon–Fri 8:30–5 💷 Inexpensive

TEREZÍN

In 1942 the Nazis turned the garrison town of Terezín into a ghetto and transit camp for Jews. More than 150,000 people were held here during the war. Most were transported to the death camp at Auschwitz, but around 35,000 died here of disease and starvation. At the same time the Nazis used Terezín for their perverted propaganda purposes, persuading Red Cross visitors that this was a flourishing cultural and commercial centre. The exhibition in the main fortress, now restored after the flood, gives an excellent if harrowing account of life in the camp, while across the river, in the lesser fortress, visitors can tour the barracks, workshops, isolation cells, mortuaries, execution grounds and mass graves.

www.pamatnik-terezin.cz

✉ Principova alej 304 ☎ 416 782 225 ⏰ Apr–Oct daily 9–6; Nov–Mar daily 9–5:30 💶 Moderate 🍴 Restaurant (£) 🚌 Coach from Praha Florenc bus station

TŘEBOŇ

The charming spa town of Třeboň is best known for the quality of its carp ponds, which date back to the 14th century – Carp Rožmberk is on the menu of many restaurants even today. Four surviving gates lead into the walled Old Town, which has at its heart a beautiful, elongated square. Dating from 1566, the Town Hall is decorated with three coats of arms: those of the town and its wealthy patrons, the Rožmberks and the Schwarzenbergs. Opposite is the 16th-century White Horse Inn, which has an unusual turreted gable. Třeboň has its own brewery and horse-drawn drays deliver Regent beer to the local hotels and restaurants. The Augustinian monastery church of St Giles dates from 1367 and contains a number of Gothic features, including a statue of the Madonna. The attractive Renaissance **château** is open to the public and was built in 1562 by the Rožmberk family.

🛈 Masarykovo náměstí 103 ☎ 384 721 169

🚉 Praha Hlavní nádraží

Château ⏰ Jun–Aug Tue–Sun 9–5:15; Tue–Sun Apr–May, Sep–Oct 9–4 💶 Moderate

Index

Acknowledgements

The Automobile Association would like to thank the following photographers and companies for their assistance in the preparation of this book. Abbreviations for the picture credits are as follows – (t) top; (b) bottom; (c) centre; (l) left; (r) right; (AA) AA World Travel Library

4l River Vltava seen from Letna, AA/Jonathan Smith; **4c** Mala Strana metro station, AA/Jon Wyand; **4r** St Vitus Cathedral, AA/Simon McBride; **5l** Waldstein Palace, AA/Clive Sawyer; **5c** Charles Bridge, AA/Simon McBride; **5r** Cesky Krumlov, AA/Jon Wyand; **6/7** River Vltava seen from Letna, AA/Jonathan Smith; **8/9** Astronomical Clock, Old Town Square, AA/Clive Sawyer; **10/11t** Old Town, AA/Simon McBride; **10bl** Male Namesti, Old Town, AA/Jonathan Smith; **10/11b** Old Town Square, AA/Jonathan Smith; **11c** Tram, AA/Jonathan Smith; **12bl** Traditional food, AA/Jonathan Smith; **12br** Old Town Square, AA/Simon McBride; **13tr** Bakery, AA/Jonathan Smith; **13b** Obecni dum, Old Town, AA/Jonathan Smith; **14l** Evropa Hotel, Wenceslas Square, AA/Jon Wyand; **14br** Pilsner Urquell lager, AA/Jon Wyand; **15tl** Cafe Imperial, New Town, AA/Jonathan Smith; **15cr** Astronomical Clock, Old Town, AA/Simon McBride; **15bl** Absinthe, AA/Jonathan Smith; **16** Charles Bridge, AA/Simon McBride; **17** Figures on astronomical clock, Old Town Square, AA/Clive Sawyer; **18tl** Beer tap, U Zlatecho tygra, AA/Simon McBride; **18/19t** Royal Gardens seen from the Belvedere, AA/Simon McBride; **18/19b** Estates Theatre, AA/Clive Sawyer; **20/21** Mala Strana metro station, AA/Jon Wyand; **24** Obecni dum, AA/Jon Wyand; **25** Old Town Square, AA/Simon McBride; **26t** Plane, Digitalvision; **27** Traffic on Jiraskuv most, AA/Jonathan Smith; **28** River Vltava, AA/Jonathan Smith; **29** Tram, AA/Jonathan Smith; **31** Telephone, AA/Simon McBride; **34/35** St Vitus and Prague Castle, AA/Simon McBride; **36b** St Nicholas, Mala Strana, AA/Tony Souter; **37t** View from Mala Strana area towards Charles Bridge, AA/Simon McBride; **38/39** Inside Spanish Synagogue, AA/Jonathan Smith; **39br** Old Jewish Cemetery, AA/Simon McBride; **40cl** St Vitus Cathedral, AA/Simon McBride; **40bl** St Vitus, AA/Tony Souter; **41t** St Vitus Cathedral, AA; **41b** Alfons Mucha window, St Vitus, AA/Jon Wyand; **42** Loreta, AA/Simon McBride; **43** Loreta, AA/Simon McBride; **44t** Prague Castle, AA/Jonathan Smith; **44c** Castle Gardens, AA/Clive Sawyer; **44/45b** Prague Castle, AA/Jonathan Smith; **45tl** Chapel of the Holy Cross, Prague Castle, AA/Clive Sawyer; **46** Astronomical clock, Old Town Square, AA/Clive Sawyer; **47** Astronomical clock, Old Town Square, AA/Simon McBride; **48** German paintings, Sternbersky palac, AA/Jonathan Smith; **50bc** Strahov Gospel, Strahov Monastery, AA/Simon McBride; **50/51** Philosophical Hall, Strahov Monastery, AA/Simon McBride; **51r** Strahov Monastery, AA/Simon McBride; **52/53** Wenceslas Square, © Yadid Levy/Alamy; **54** Veletrzni Palac, AA/Jonathan Smith; **55/56** Atrium view, Veletrzni Palac, AA/Jonathan Smith; **56/57** Waldstein Palace, AA/Clive Sawyer; **58/59** Painting, Municipal Museum, AA/Jonathan Smith; **60** U Kalicha, AA/Tony Souter; **62/63** Czech beer © Chris Frederiksson/Alamy; **64/65** View from Petrin Hill, AA/Clive Sawyer; **66** Tyn Church, Old Town Square, AA/Simon McBride; **67** Nerudova street, AA/Jonathan Smith; **68/69** Cernin Palace, AA/Clive Sawyer; **70/71** St Nicholas Church, Old Town, AA/Simon McBride; **73** Wooden toys, AA/Jonathan Smith; **74** Gardens beneath Prague Castle, AA/Simon McBride; **76** Aria Hotel; **78** Bata shop window, AA/Jonathan Smith; **80/81** Charles Bridge, AA/Simon McBride; **83** Old Town Square, AA/Jonathan Smith; **85** Bethlehem Chapel, AA/Tony Souter; **86t** Black Madonna House, AA/Jonathan Smith; **86c** Black Madonna in her cage, AA/Clive Sawyer; **87b** House at the Stone Bell, AA/Jon Wyand; **88** Charles Bridge, AA/Jonathan Smith; **89** Karolinum, AA/Clive Sawyer; **90** Library, Klementinum, AA/Jonathan Smith; **91** Klementinum, AA/Jonathan Smith; **92** Charles IV, Knights of the Cross Square, AA/Simon McBride; **93** St Saviour, Knights of the Cross Square, AA/Simon McBride; **94/95t** River Vltava and Smetana Museum (on left), AA/Simon McBride; **94b** Bedrich Smetana statue, AA/Jon Wyand; **96t** Old Town Square, AA/Simon McBride; **96b** Jan Hus monument, AA/Jon Wyand; **97** Estates Theatre, AA/Jon Wyand; **98t** Ungelt, AA/Jonathan Smith; **98b** Wine Shop Ungelt, AA/Jonathan Smith; **107** St George's Convent and Basilica, AA/Jonathan Smith; **108** Memorial to the Battle of the White Mountain, AA/Jon Wyand; **109** Benedicitine Monastery of Brevnov, AA/Jon Wyand; **110** Cernin Palace, AA/Jon Wyand; **111b** Kafka Museum, © Yadid Levy/Alamy; **112** Schwartzenberg Palace, AA/Clive Sawyer; **113t** Basilica of St George, AA/Jon Wyand; **113b** St. George's Convent, AA/Jonathan Smith; **114** Church of Our Lady of Victory, AA/Tony Souter; **115** Spire, Church of St Thomas, AA/Clive Sawyer; **116t** The Royal Gardens, AA/Simon McBride; **116b** Singing Fountain, Royal Gardens, AA/Simon McBride; **117** Lapidarium, AA/Clive Sawyer; **118** John Lennon Wall, AA/Jon Wyand; **119** Malostranske namesti, AA/Simon McBride; **120/121** Nerudova, AA/Jon Wyand; **122** Cerninska street, Novy Svet, AA/Jon Wyand; **123** Church of St Lawrence, Kinsky Garden, Petrin Hill, AA/Jon Wyand; **124** Certovka, AA/Simon McBride; **125** Lesser Quarter, AA/Simon McBride; **126t** Troja Chateau, AA/Clive Sawyer; **126c** Troja Chateau, AA/Jon Wyand; **127** Waldstein Gardens, AA/Clive Sawyer; **128** Exhibition Hall, Vystaviste, AA/Clive Sawyer; **129** Golden Lane, AA/Simon McBride; **134** Old-New Synagogue, AA/Simon McBride; **135t** Church of Sv. Salvator, St Agnes's Convent, AA/Jonathan Smith; **135b** Altarpiece "Resurrection" by the Master of the Trebon, St Agnes's Convent, AA/Jonathan Smith; **136/137** St Nicholas Church, AA/Simon McBride; **139** Maiselova Synagoga, AA/Jonathan Smith; **140** Ceremonial Hall, AA/Tony Souter; **141** Pinkas Synagogue, AA/Jonathan Smith; **142** Old-New Synagogue, AA/Jon Wyand; **143** Old Jewish Cemetery, AA/Tony Souter; **144** Prague Museum of Decorative Arts, AA/Jon Wyand; **147** Church of St Cyril and St Methodius, AA/Jonathan Smith; **148t** Church of Our Lady of the Snows, AA/Jon Wyand; **148b** Memorial to the parachutists, Church of SS Cyril and Methodius, AA/Clive Sawyer; **150** Old Town Square in winter (1862) painting by Ferdinand Lepie, Muzeum Hlavniho Mesta Prahy, AA/Jonathan Smith; **151** Bust of Stalin, Museum of Communism, AA/Jonathan Smith; **153** National Theatre, AA/Jonathan Smith; **154** Radio Free Europe Building, AA Jonathan Smith; **155** Obecni Dum, AA/Simon McBride; **157** Powder Tower, AA/Clive Sawyer; **158** Church of St Peter and St Paul,

AA/Clive Sawyer; **164/165** Cesky Krumlov, AA/Jon Wyand; **167** Brno, AA/Jon Wyand; **168** Church of St Peter and Paul, Melnik, AA/Jon Wyand; **169t** Town Hall, Melnik, AA/Jon Wyand; **171** Cesky Krumlov, AA/Jon Wyand; **172b** Hradec Kralove, AA/J Wyand; **172/173c** Karlovy Vary, AA/Jon Wyand; **174** Karlstejn Castle, AA/Clive Sawyer; **176** Kutna Hora, AA/Jon Wyand; **178** Melnik, AA/Jon Wyand; **179** Plzen, AA/Jon Wyand; **180/181** Equestrian statue of Jan Zizka, Tabor, AA/Jon Wyand; **182** Gravestones, Terezin, AA/Jon Wyand.

Every effort has been made to trace the copyright holders, and we apologise in advance for any accidental errors. We would be happy to apply the corrections in the following edition of this publication.

Street index

Site locator index

This index relates to the maps on the covers. We have given map
references to the main sights in the book. Some sights may not
be plotted on the maps.

AAA Questionnaire

Dear Traveler

Your comments, opinions and recommendations are very important to us. So please help us to improve our travel guides by taking a few minutes to complete this simple questionnaire.

Send to: Essential Guides,
MailStop 64, 1000 AAA Drive, Heathrow, FL 32746–5063

Your recommendations...

We always encourage readers' recommendations for restaurants, nightlife or shopping – if your recommendation is added to the next edition of the guide, we will send you a FREE AAA Essential Guide of your choice. Please state below the establishment name, location and your reasons for recommending it.

_____

_____

_____

_____

Please send me AAA Essential _____

About this guide...

Which title did you buy?

_____ **AAA Essential**

Where did you buy it? _____

When? m m / y y

Why did you choose a AAA Essential Guide? _____

_____

_____

Did this guide meet with your expectations?

Exceeded ☐   Met all ☐   Met most ☐   Fell below ☐

Please give your reasons _____

_____

_____

continued on next page...

Were there any aspects of this guide that you particularly liked? _____

_____

_____

_____

_____

Is there anything we could have done better? _____

_____

_____

_____

_____

About you...
Name (Mr/Mrs/Ms) _____

Address _____

_____ **Zip** _____

Daytime tel nos. _____

Which age group are you in?
Under 25 ☐   25–34 ☐   35–44 ☐   45–54 ☐   55–64 ☐   65+ ☐

How many trips do you make a year?
Less than one ☐   One ☐   Two ☐   Three or more ☐

Are you a AAA member? Yes ☐   No ☐

Name of AAA club _____

About your trip
When did you book? m m / y y   **When did you travel?** m m / y y

How long did you stay? _____

Was it for business or leisure? _____

Did you buy any other travel guides for your trip? Yes ☐   No ☐

If yes, which ones? _____

_____

Thank you for taking the time to complete this questionnaire.